THIS NAKED LIFE

THIS NAKED LIFE

48 True Stories of Finding Freedom from Alcohol

Edited by Annie Grace

Copyright © 2020 This Naked Mind, LLC. All rights reserved.

Library of Congress Control Number: 2020911277

ISBN: 978-0-9967150-3-4

No part of this publication may be reproduced, stored in a retrieval system, or transmitted, in any form or by any means, electronic, mechanical, photocopying, recording, or otherwise without the prior permission of the publishers.

While all stories are authentic and written by real people, some names have been changed.

Editing by Quill Pen Editorial Services

Cover Design by Mary Purdie

You agree that This Naked Mind, LLC is not comprised of licensed medical or psychological professionals and the information presented herein is for informational and educational purposes only and is not intended to diagnose, treat, cure, or prevent any disease. The information is in no way intended as medical advice, substance-abuse counseling, psychological counseling, or as a substitute for medical or any other professional counseling. The information should be used in conjunction with the guidance and care of a physician. Consult a physician before using the information in this book. You agree your use of the information in this book is at your own risk and that This Naked Mind, LLC does not guarantee results.

This Naked Mind, LLC provides the contents of this book on an "AS IS" basis and disclaims all representations and warranties, express or implied, including the warranty of merchantability and warranty for a particular purpose. You hereby release This Naked Mind, LLC, its managers, members, employees, and agents for any damages whatsoever arising out of or in connection with your use of this book, including indirect, incidental, special, punitive, or consequential damages to the fullest extent permitted by law. Your use of this book confirms your agreement to the above terms and conditions.

This book is dedicated to the very people who wrote it.

The brave, the vulnerable, and the courageous
who have shared a piece of themselves in these pages.

Stories heal. And thanks to you,
this book is full to the brim of healing, life-giving words.

Reach out. We are here for you.

ThisNakedMind.com
TheAlcoholExperiment.com

Email: hello@thisnakedmind.com
Instagram: @thisnakedmind
Facebook: This Naked Mind
Twitter: @thisnakedmind

TABLE OF CONTENTS

Introduction 1

A Mosaic of Freedom 3
  Simone's Story

A Semicolon Tattoo 8
  John's Story

Take That, Subconscious Dave 13
  Diane's Story

An Apple Fresh Off the Tree 18
  Cheryl's Story

The Train I'm On 23
  Wyatt's Story

If It Can Happen to Me 30
  Raegan's Story

Healing Myself 37
  Erin's Story

Until It Wasn't 43
  Becca's Story

How to Fall in Love Again 48
  Ryan and Alison's Story

Taking a Break 56
  Pamela's Story

The Power of a Science-Based Approach 62
  Hannah's Story

The Day I Couldn't Get Drunk 66
  Mike J.'s Story

Feeling Grown-Up 71
  Nancy's Story

Living Honestly 76
  Meagan's Story

Finding Healing from C-PTSD 81
  Terrance's Story

Full Circle 87
Kate's Story

After Forty Years 91
Lesley's Story

The Very Worst Christmas 95
Rob's Story

Sorry, I Got Drunk 99
Elizabeth's Story

It Really Doesn't Suck 104
Scott's Story

Surgically Removed 109
Jennifer's Story

Dragged Down 113
Lisa B.'s Story

The People That We Are 119
Lorraine's Story

Nobody Knew But Me 124
Grace's Story

Hunted By Fear 129
Carolyn's Story

I Just Didn't Want to Drink Poison Anymore 133
Marc's Story

11,000 Calories and £240 138
Ria's Story

One Hundred Percent Me 142
Laura's Story

A Safe Presence 146
Brandy's Story

When the Excuses Felt Hollow 153
Simon's Story

I Started to Heal 157
Emma's Story

Voted "Least Likely to Ever Quit Drinking" 161
Alex's Story

From Drinking to Fit In to Drinking to Get By 166
Amanda's Story

I Wasn't In Control 172
Christine's Story

Do You Remember?..179
  Melissa's Story

A Life-Giving Health Journey..186
  Harvey's Story

Sending My Liver on Holiday 191
  Marietta's Story

Not Another Self-Help Book..198
  Bryan's Story

A Thousand Questions 202
  Lorna's Story

My Last Hangover 207
  Lisa M.'s Story

I Just Don't Want To..212
  Andrew's Story

This Naked Mind and Tea 216
  Stephanie's Story

I Have a Choice..220
  Robbie's Story

Quitting Cold Turkey 226
  Mike S.'s Story

Young, Wild, and Stuck 233
  L's Story

No Anesthesia..238
  Gerri's Story

A Self-Improvement Junkie..243
  AJ's Story

It Ends Here...249
  Kari's Story

Conclusion...254

THIS NAKED LIFE

INTRODUCTION

I knew I wasn't in control of my drinking, but the only time I was brave enough to admit it was when I was alone, in the dark, at three in the morning. I didn't even realize I'd begun to isolate myself—a toxic way I tried to cope with the crippling shame. Looking back, I think I pushed people away because I already *felt* alone.

Alcohol ensnares people in a web of addiction because it's an addictive substance. But it's even more insidious than that—it also cuts us off from each other. Millions of people are suffering in silence because it's scary to ask, "Am I drinking too much?"

But I wasn't alone. And neither are you.

When I started openly questioning my drinking, I expected to face judgment and stigma. Instead, I found that addressing alcohol honestly, in the bright light of day, broke down walls. Vulnerability connects us, allowing us to feel a weight lift as we say, "You too? I thought I was the only one."

Hearing others' stories is one of the most powerful ways of opening up to new possibilities, learning about ourselves and the people around us, fostering empathy, and catalyzing transformation. Stories show us that others have walked this road before us and that we, too, can achieve victory. On top of all this, it has been scientifically shown that stories trigger the same area of the brain as does actually experiencing an event! Stories literally prime our brains for our own breakthroughs.

In this book, you will find a collection of inspiring and real stories from relatable humans in all walks of life—think your neighbor, your mother, your brother, your child, the clerk at your local food market—and their beautiful and sometimes heart-wrenching quests for freedom.

I compiled these stories because I have seen the power and effect they have had on people over and over again. I am so excited to share them with you! As you read through them, you will be moved, you will be shaped, and you will be transformed. You will see living proof that you are not alone. That there is hope. That freedom is yours for the taking.

As we journey alongside those who have reclaimed control in their relationship with alcohol, we learn that the first step is to put down the weapons of shame, blame, and guilt. You must give up the fight against yourself and allow and accept what is going on within you as a perfectly normal response to an addictive substance. These accounts show, time and time again, that once we learn more about the true nature of alcohol and begin to see that we have been doing the best we could with the tools we were given, we can find love and acceptance for ourselves and anyone else who is struggling. From this place of understanding and empathy, real, easy, lasting change is possible—and these stories show how.

Whether you are reading this as you explore your own relationship with alcohol or because you're trying to better understand someone you love, find yourself a comfy place and get ready to be touched by these powerful accounts of people's journeys with *This Naked Mind*.

With so much love,
Annie Grace

A MOSAIC OF FREEDOM
Simone's Story

By the time my parents had me—in 1961, in middle America—there was already a lot of drama and trauma going on, and I think I internalized that. My dad was in the air force, and he married my mom, who was German, while he was stationed abroad in Germany. They had my two sisters there, and then he got stationed in the United States. My older sister was just six weeks old when they came back. Three months after they arrived, my dad was diagnosed with a leg sarcoma. At the time, standard treatment was to amputate the leg at the hip. He was gone, recovering in a VA hospital, for a whole year. Soon after, they got pregnant with me. And my dad's coping mechanism was drinking alcohol. That meant alcohol was always present in my household, from before I can remember. I always saw my dad drinking a lot.

My mom, meanwhile, was still recovering from her own trauma. She'd grown up in Germany during World War II, and the place she'd lived was the third most heavily bombed town in the country. She told those stories a lot, and in some ways, it almost felt like I'd lived them alongside her. That her story became mine. Sometimes pain gets passed down through generations.

I started dabbling in alcohol when I was thirteen. The first time,

I didn't like it—no surprise, since I started with Everclear, which is so strong it's now illegal in some states. I drank with my friends sometimes, but it wasn't yet something I sought out when I was alone.

Then, when I was fourteen, I was raped by a group of boys at my junior high. There was a trial and a conviction, but it didn't feel like justice. School wasn't a safe place for me anymore. The perpetrators' friends bullied me relentlessly. I asked my mom if I could switch schools, but that wasn't going to happen. This was the '70s, when you learned to deal with the cards life had dealt you. Instead, I dropped out of school, got a job, and moved in with my first boyfriend. After two years, we broke up, and my parents didn't know what to do with me. They'd recently divorced, and my dad was still drinking. My dad ended up setting me up in an apartment, and I found myself on my own at age sixteen. By this time, I was drinking and smoking pot to cope with my sense of abandonment, to forget what was going on in my life. But I was always able to take care of myself. I learned a lot, and I learned it quick.

I met my first husband when I was seventeen. He was nine years older than me, and I thought I'd found someone who would finally be my caretaker and provider. We became pregnant, and I had a baby and settled into married life. But my fairytale expectations were quickly dashed—it turned out that I was the stronger, steadier, more resourceful one in that relationship. For a few years, we managed, partying with friends to forget the misery. Ten years later, we had our second son.

And then I got tired of it. I decided I wanted something more. I enrolled in nursing school and graduated in 1994—I've been a nurse ever since—and two years later, I divorced my first husband. But I was still drinking, and I drank to get drunk, to obliviate myself.

I was single for five years, and during this time, my drinking increased even though I was productive and moving forward.

Ultimately, it was a coping mechanism that helped me avoid dealing with the real sources of trauma in my life.

The world moved on, and I moved with it. I met my now-husband, and we've been together for twenty years. We drank socially with friends, and he's in an industry where alcohol plays a big role. As we went to more and more of these alcohol-soaked events, my need for alcohol kept growing. I'd become conditioned to it. Little by little, I started questioning my drinking habits. My husband made comments about it, too—he can have a drink or two and stop, and it's not an issue for him. He didn't grow up drinking in the way I did.

Then, an *aha* moment. We liked to watch Anthony Bourdain. After Bourdain's death, they found a lot of alcohol in his blood. No drugs, but a lot of alcohol. That really got me thinking. Soon after, I saw *This Naked Mind* and downloaded it to my Kindle. It made so much sense to me. I appreciated that it was written from a biopsychosocial perspective, because that's how I was trained as a nurse, and the rigorous science convinced me. Before that, I'd always tried to moderate, but after I got the book, I just stopped. Right then and there as I read. I didn't need to go back. *This Naked Mind* gave me permission to say that my struggles with alcohol weren't because of a personal weakness. That addiction has a biological cause because of natural neurochemical reactions.

I'm happy to say I haven't had a drink since. I don't have to do that anymore. I got off that train. We still sometimes go to alcohol-soaked events, but they don't trouble me. I've found that if I have a drink in my hand, nobody ever says anything. So I just go straight to the bar or ask a server for soda and lime. I still have just as good a time.

I'm sleeping better, looking better, eating better. My relationships are improving, and I have more energy. I'm paying more attention to my needs and my health. I'm turning down invitations to parties I don't want to go to. I'm giving myself permission to be an introvert—because that's who I really am. For a little while, I took 5-HTP—an amino acid that's a precursor to serotonin—but I didn't need it for long. It just helped me bridge the gap during the physical transition period.

Now, in this place of contentment and freedom, I look back at my younger self and wish I could tell her that the peace and harmony she seeks is on the other side of quitting. That she's done hard, brave things before and always risen to the occasion. And that the growth and self-respect and confidence she'll have—especially in showing other people how to treat her—makes it all worth it a hundredfold. I can't talk to younger Simone—not really—but I can tell my story to others and hope that it resonates, becoming a small part of this movement that's changing so many lives. I'm ordinarily a private person, but I felt so strongly about sharing this. Because when I listen to other people's stories, I find a little piece of myself in each of them—like I'm a mosaic. And I hope that, by telling this story, other people can find a piece of themselves in it too.

"You are strong, and by making your commitment you have already won."

—Annie Grace, *This Naked Mind*

A SEMICOLON TATTOO
John's Story

November 21.

Pain sears into my wrist as the tattoo artist etches a semicolon onto my right arm—my drinking arm. It's time to stop drinking. When the tattoo is finished, I walk to the microbrewery across the street for a final farewell. I savor the taste of the beer. This is my last drink ever.

It's like saying goodbye to a friend, but it feels so good to bury that friend before it buries me.

Months later, I look back on that day with the most profound sense of relief. I'm taking the time to write this out, to go public with my story, in hopes that I might bring someone comfort and that even a single person would give some thought to changing their drinking habits.

I got out just in time. The sparks had caught flame, but the house hadn't yet burned down around me. After years and years of abusing my body with alcohol, I feel much gratitude that I've found a way to live without it. I honestly did not think it would be possible in my lifetime.

Like a lot of people, I started drinking my senior year in high school. Alcohol was my constant companion for thirty-four years.

Of course, I never thought it was a problem. It never affected my work life, and I didn't drink in the morning.

After all, shouldn't I be rewarded for working hard?

But the truth was, I was a terrible binge drinker and would find anything in the house to drink. If I was out of beer (not that wimpy lite beer—IPAs with seven to eight percent alcohol, sixteen ounces at a time, instead of twelve), I would turn to wine and then hard liquor. Sometimes, I would have hard liquor first and then wine!

I even organized my social life and my friendships around alcohol. When friends invited me out, I weighed my options based on where I could drink the most alcohol and get away with it. They didn't know I was struggling, because alcohol was part of the setting—it was the common denominator, the thing we were all doing together. They didn't know I'd been counting down the minutes all day until the first buzz of IPA warmed my throat, that I'd been desperate for work to end and for "happy hour" to arrive.

I tried to stop drinking twice before, on the advice of my doctor, therapist, and wife. I thought it would be all about willpower. Both attempts lasted about seven months and were terribly painful. I was mad that I was being denied the ability to drink.

Eventually, I eased my way back into alcohol because "I am a man, and I should be able to handle a drink." First just on the weekends, then only the last part of the week and the weekends (after all, I'd earned it), and then every day. Each time I got in deeper than before because I thought I needed to "catch up" for the time lost not drinking. You know the story—maybe you've lived it—but it's cathartic to write it out.

Everything changed when I read *This Naked Mind*. I knew I was running out of time, that I had to stop or my life would spiral out of control. But after two agonizing attempts at quitting—and the subsequent failures—it seemed overwhelming. My patient, loving wife and I have had many "discussions" about my alcohol consumption, and she could never truly understand what I was doing to my body, why I couldn't quit. It got to the point where I still chose alcohol over everything else—even at the cost of possibly losing my wife. I tried to hide it, desperately thinking I deserved to be able to drink as much as I wanted.

I wish I could remember where I first stumbled over the book on social media, but I decided to stop drinking—for good this time—when I was about halfway through reading it. That was November 21. And it was just in time—before I spiraled out of control and lost the most important things in my life. I am sure I would not have been granted too many more—if any—reboots of my broken promises to stop drinking.

This has been nothing like my earlier ill-fated attempts at quitting. It's been great! Even though I was skeptical about its claim to affect my subconscious—I find that stuff hard to believe—it changed my thinking and my drinking. I've celebrated holidays—Thanksgiving, Christmas, even New Year's—completely sober and haven't missed drinking at all, even though those holidays have usually been an excuse to let loose. But the most meaningful day was my son's twenty-first birthday.

You see, for years I'd looked forward to drinking with him, just like I did with my daughter when she turned twenty-one. I couldn't wait to drink with both of them, which sounds so silly now. I've been very open with both my children about what I've been dealing with and about my worries of how genetics might play into their decisions regarding alcohol.

I've worried about how my habits might affect their choices—they've seen me passed out on the floor a few times. And yet, I'd wanted this moment of drinking with my son.

But my son's twenty-first birthday came after November 21—after my realization that alcohol wasn't making my life better and that I didn't want it anymore. On his birthday, my wife and I visited him at college and took him and his friends out to dinner.

Even though we offered to buy them drinks, he chose not to drink. When we asked why, he said, "Because I drove to the restaurant."

I was so proud of him, so impressed with his mature decision, especially because I am well aware of what happens in college. It's where I perfected my craft. Now that I'm sober and able to change my thinking about the possibility of living without drinking, I have confidence in my children's decisions around alcohol. They've seen me pass out drunk, but they've also seen me defeat it.

I've found out a lot about myself lately: depression for the last five years (and probably a lot longer), seasonal affective disorder (SAD) two years later, and adult ADHD a few months ago. It's funny—I had convinced myself that I enjoyed drinking, but the depression was a roller coaster when alcohol was in my life. Now it's so much better. I'm on proper medication now, too, and I feel at ease and more stable. Not only do I not crave alcohol—I don't need it to numb the pain.

My whole life has changed since that beautiful day.

When I trace the semicolon tattoo on my wrist, the relief and gratitude well up in me all over again. The marking is a permanent reminder of how far I've come—that I escaped the burning building just in time. And that brings me to today, as I share my story for someone else who needs it.

I got out. And as I think of all I've gained, a simple refrain runs through my mind, the words "thank you" repeating over and over again, every time I look down at that tattoo.

"There are a million reasons why I am happier now, but above all I know myself. I feel comfortable and confident in my own skin. I love being alive, love being me. This is true happiness."

—Annie Grace, *This Naked Mind*

TAKE THAT, SUBCONSCIOUS DAVE
Diane's Story

I was pretty sure my future involved me dying alone with dementia, alienated from the daughter I adored and my precious grandchildren, because—as my ever-helpful ex-husband had repeatedly pointed out—I ruined everything. And this turn of events would be my fault, because I was so damn weak and pathetic where alcohol was concerned. Because despite a hundred promises to stop drinking, every night found me at the store, buying yet another bottle of wine.

I knew I had a real problem, but I was still being very disciplined. I mean, I only bought a single bottle of wine every night. Obviously that made me much better off than those who bought multiple bottles.

At age sixty-one, the best I could see for myself was a former nurse practitioner, one with multiple degrees and a great mind, dying with a fried brain. With all that brain power and logic, I couldn't figure out how I'd let this happen or why I couldn't stop drinking.

It hadn't always been this way. I knew what alcohol could do to a person—I'd seen it consume my father throughout my childhood—so much so that I wouldn't go drinking on the trolley tracks with my high school friends before the football games. I met up with them later instead, ignoring the taunts that I was a "goody two-shoes" or a "prude" and deciding that I didn't care, that I'd be smart, successful, and accomplished.

And I was!

By college, I'd left behind my careful attitude toward alcohol because I just knew I was too smart to get caught up in it. I drank—at times too much—but it was just something I did, something that was fun, something that felt good when that fuzzy numbness entered from the sides of my eyes, making everything soft and out of focus.

My caution and my brain never prepared me for marrying a narcissist. That man was so charming, so warm, so loving, and smart! Everyone told me how marvelous he was, how loved I was, and how lucky I was to have him in my life. And I just couldn't figure out why I did things to make him so mad at me, not just once in a while but every single day.

But I was nothing but determined, and I was sure I could logically figure it out. Each morning, I pledged to be better, more loving, more kind, and more respectful, so he would be happy with me. I just failed daily.

In the late 1990s, I found out he was cheating on me—again.

The first time had just been a mistake of circumstances, I was sure.

This time, I pulled a bottle of Zinfandel out of the refrigerator, while playing the soundtrack from *City of Angels*, and decided the best course of action was to numb all the pain.

And it worked!

And so my career with alcohol was launched.

I didn't drink all the time, but I started doing something I'd never done—I began to sneak alcohol, grabbing a swallow here and there. When we finally divorced in 2015—apparently, I was determined to figure out my marriage for all those years—I was into full-blown nightly consumption, blackouts and all. I was a solitary drinker, content with my bottle of wine.

At least I knew what to expect.

Only problem was guilt and shame over my habit consumed me. And I couldn't figure out how to stop. I knew I would never go to AA and declare in front of anyone that I was an alcoholic. So I tried online groups. I tried vitamin supplements through a program in Minnesota. Swallowed almost fifty pills a day to "cure" myself.

Yeah, that didn't work.

And one day, I saw a Facebook post for This Naked Mind. Intrigued, I ordered a course. At least I wouldn't be counting vitamins. I did it for a week and thought Annie Grace might have something here . . . and then I set it aside to think about. And I did think about it for the next fifteen months, while I continued drinking.

Finally, I saw an announcement that a This Naked Mind live event was coming to a city near me. Maybe seeing Annie Grace in person would help. So I went.

It was marvelous! The message was amazing—it wasn't my fault! I could learn to stop drinking! All I had to do was change my thought patterns! And I actually was able to tell these people I drank too much, and they didn't run screaming from the room! I cried so much one eye became swollen shut! I was sure I had it! And I did!

For ten days.

On the eleventh, I decided to reward myself with a Manhattan cocktail, and then a second, and then a third, and . . . wait, who's counting?

Turns out that thinking about changing wasn't enough. It actually required work, concentration, practice, and connection with others.

Who knew?

So when the thirty-day Live Alcohol Experiment launched the

next January, I was all in. I was going to do this, and nothing was going to stop me.

Finally.

My last drink was actually December 30 because I didn't want to enter the New Year with any alcohol in my system at all. I listened to the videos daily and drew support from others in the program. And I told myself I deserve a life without alcohol.

I learned about my subconscious and the dopamine surge alcohol gave me. I named my subconscious Dave and had discussions with him when he told me to drink. At times, I told him to shut the eff up—and he would! After thirty days alcohol-free, I decided to go into the intensive course to help cement my thoughts and maintain my connections with others.

I had friends, I was sleeping, I looked great, and my mind was working—and I preferred to keep it that way.

So cement it I did!

My ex-husband really was wrong. I don't ruin everything. I can change, I can unlearn things, and I can have a marvelous life where I feel the whole range of emotions, from despair to joy. I am so much more than a bottle of wine. Through *This Naked Mind*, I found the path back to me—and kinda like those ruby slippers, it turned out I'd had the ability the whole time; I just needed to be shown how to do it.

So now I do it daily.

Alcohol-free me has a great life and a great future.

Take that, Subconscious Dave.

"I thought I was alone. I thought I was the only one who was questioning my drinking habits. Nothing could be further from the truth!"

—Annie Grace, *The Alcohol Experiment*

AN APPLE FRESH OFF THE TREE
Cheryl's Story

The day before I stopped drinking, I woke up with a hangover. I was thirty-five years old and caring for my one-year-old son, and I hadn't even felt like I had a buzz at the wedding I'd attended the night before. When my son started to cry himself awake, I peeled myself out of bed, wishing I could sleep longer. But if I relinquished the chore to my husband, I'd have to admit—at least to myself—that I couldn't handle my relationship with alcohol. That wasn't a notion I was ready to face.

With my son in tow, I dragged myself to the grocery store to shop for the upcoming week. I picked up three bottles of Bloody Mary mix but forgot the bread. Once I got home, I fixed myself a Bloody Mary while I did the chores—unpacking the groceries, making lunches for the week, doing laundry. I poured a second and a third to make the chores and the thought of work the next day more bearable.

So that I could call myself a good mother, I brought the baby outside to pick some apples in the cool, crisp fall air. Then I poured myself a pint of craft beer from our Kegerator—something I was very proud to own. I set my beer down and lifted the baby to the tree. He snapped off an apple, and as he settled his little teeth into the fruit's skin, his face beamed with pure delight. From an apple. He didn't need alcohol to feel joy, so why did I?

I finished two or three more beers and then switched to wine because the beer was starting to fill me up. Dread curled in my stomach at the thought of work the next day. Surely alcohol could numb that feeling.

The next morning, the day I stopped drinking, I woke up to my 5:15 a.m. alarm and, like most mornings, ran through all the excuses I could think of to call in sick. I always dragged myself out of bed anyway, because calling in would mean I had an alcohol problem. That still wasn't something I could admit. To combat my hangover, I grabbed a Pedialyte, which I kept stocked in the pantry—not for my child but for me and my constant hangovers.

I grabbed my phone from the charger and saw that my husband had sent me a video. When I hit play, I saw my lifeless body lying across the couch. My husband's hand was pulling up my arm and letting it fall, over and over again. He kept calling my name and saying it was time to go to bed, but it was clear I wasn't waking up.

I tried to remember the night before. I didn't remember going to bed at all—if I'd brushed my teeth, taken my medication, or checked on the baby. After finishing the video, I contritely walked into the kitchen, where my husband was eating breakfast.

"Thanks for the video," I murmured.

"That wasn't even the best part," he said. "All of a sudden, you flew up off the couch, ran into the nursery, and started yelling that it was time for the beach, and that we had to go now. I had to pull you out of the room."

I didn't remember any of it.

When I headed out to work, I bought a greasy bacon, egg, and cheese breakfast sandwich to absorb some of the previous day's alcohol. I hadn't even felt drunk the evening before. Why was I doing this? If I didn't even feel the alcohol when I was drinking but still felt like complete crap the day after, what was the point? Why was I even trying to get drunk, anyway?

With these questions pulsing in time with my headache, I started digging around on the internet and stumbled upon *This Naked Mind*. I started reading and found myself blown away. The book had answers to the questions that had been plaguing me all day. When we drink, the pleasure center in our brain, the nucleus accumbens, is artificially stimulated, giving us that twenty-minute high. Stimulation of dopamine, the "learning" molecule, makes us feel good, telling our brain to say, "Keep doing what you're doing." However, to maintain homeostasis, our brain then releases dynorphin, a chemical downer. When the alcohol wears off, we're left feeling more down than when we started drinking. So we beat ourselves up for partaking in the drinks . . . and then grab another drink to numb our feelings of disgust and to soothe the itch.

There wasn't anything wrong with me, I realized, feeling suddenly free. It wasn't that I had an alcohol problem. It was that alcohol was working exactly as it was designed to do. In a single day, my desire for alcohol completely shifted.

That was day one of an alcohol-free life.

Since I quit drinking, I've learned that chores don't feel like chores if I think about them as planning a healthy week for myself and my loved ones. Completing tasks that my family depends on me for can actually feel good—it can be a natural release of dopamine. I've realized that I don't have to dread work if I'm not showing up with a hangover. In fact, I can think of work as adult time where I can have conversations with coworkers, drink my coffee while it's hot, and go to the bathroom in private without worrying that my toddler is licking an electrical socket.

Weekends can be spent enjoying activities with my family and friends, not consumed with the thought of where my next drink will come from. I now don't have to worry about not being able to drive in the evening because I've been drinking. I can just go where I need to go—it's so freeing.

Most poignantly, I notice little things that I've never noticed before. I'm more aware and present. I think of how delighted my son is when he tastes an apple fresh off the tree. An apple doesn't have a lick of alcohol in it, and it brings him such joy. I can see, with a clear mind, the difference between pure joy and artificial stimulation. As Annie Grace wrote, "Just because laughing gas makes you giggly doesn't mean it brings you happiness."

"*Without desire, there is no temptation. Without temptation, there is no addiction.*"

—Annie Grace, *This Naked Mind*

THE TRAIN I'M ON
Wyatt's Story

I woke up on a stretcher in a bright hallway, a sour whisper of whiskey in the back of my throat and a dull, rhythmic throbbing in my temples. I rolled over.

"Hello?" I said.

The nurses congregating at a nearby desk paused their conversation, regarding me with a combination of boredom and annoyance.

"You can go whenever you're ready," one of them said, not even looking up from her clipboard. "Your partner left your stuff with you."

I looked down and saw vomit on my shirt and a hospital bracelet on my wrist, saw my stupid Halloween costume balled up by my legs—a flight suit. I was, for a brief and very unheroic stint earlier in the night, a fighter pilot. I remembered hazy flashes—friends gathered around a fire pit while I puked, slumped over on the ground with my aviator sunglasses beside me; my partner Mary helping me up the stairs while whispering words of encouragement: *You're OK, you're OK, you just drank too much*; being loaded into the back of an ambulance.

"Is she still here?" I asked the nurses.

"No," another one said gruffly. "Visitors aren't allowed to stay back here. She left hours ago."

I had to get myself together. This wasn't me. I was successful, funny, and charming. "Got a little too crazy last night," I said brightly, gathering my stuff. "Halloween, right?"

They didn't bother to answer me this time. *Got a little too crazy last night?* Who was I, a frat boy on a bender?

I looked at the name printed on my bracelet. It didn't include my title—professor, doctor. Thirty-five-year-old Wyatt, waking up alone in an ER. Just another drunk in the hospital on Halloween.

Stories about alcohol always start like this, don't they? They start in the darkest black of night, at rock bottom, in the hospital, on the street. They never start with the soft pop of a cork, marking the opening of an evening full of delightful possibility, or on a patio in the afternoon while drinking sweating margaritas, laughing with grad school friends. But the darkness encroaches so gently and so slowly that by the time you're lost in it, it feels like you've always been there.

It becomes the only part of the story you can remember.

It's like you were on a train that entered a tunnel you didn't see coming, because you can't see what's just ahead of you when you're on a train; you can only see the scenery sweeping by beside you, what seems normal, what seems like the inevitability of life.

I remember calling my partner as I left the hospital that day. This was the second hospital visit in five months. I heard a new edge of exhaustion in her voice with only a thin veneer of concern.

"We'll talk about it when you get home," she said.

I didn't blame her. This was what I did.

I'd sulked at Mary's shows, getting blackout drunk when I should have been watching her enchant sold-out crowds hanging on her every word. I got anxious being around her fans—I loved them, but there was pressure that came with being Mary Lambert's partner at a big event.

We both have bipolar disorder—a big part of her work is dismantling stigma around mental health. I don't know if my drinking behavior started as a way of self-medicating the bipolar disorder or not, but I wasn't interested in alcohol until grad school. Back then, I was in a really terrible, abusive relationship—that, I'm sure, I was self-medicating. It started out with champagne and wine, and gradually I fell in love with alcohol. I got to the point where I was drinking a fifth of whiskey every other day and a minimum of five beers a night.

At various points in my life, I made attempts to cut back on drinking or to make little rules for myself—which I now know is super common. I'd say, "I'm not going to drink hard liquor anymore" or "Oh, actually, I'm just not going to drink brown liquor—that was the problem" or "I guess I just can't have wine."

But I didn't realize how bad it had gotten until after I met Mary. Our partnership had been the best and healthiest relationship of my life, but for the first year, I only saw it and its possibilities through the fog of drinking. I did things drunk that haunted me sober—I drove while intoxicated, struggling to summon the alertness necessary to keep me from getting pulled over or killing someone. I picked needless, ridiculous fights with Mary, treating her horribly. I said hurtful things I never remembered saying, reliving them through her heartbreaking reenactments during those dreadful mornings while I was hungover.

As awful as it must have been for her, Mary never confronted me about my drinking. She'd cut way back on her own alcohol use, so she knew that controlling my drinking was a journey I'd have to take when I was ready for it. She couldn't force me to change, and she knew change wouldn't stick if she pushed it on me. She just supported me, and I'm so grateful for that.

But I had entered the tunnel; I knew it.

The need for change was thrown into sharp relief when Mary's sister came to visit us. As always, I was drinking way more than everyone else. I don't even remember what I was doing—dancing around and acting like an idiot in the living room, I guess. I was really drunk, but just sober enough to hear Mary turn to her sister and say, "I'm going to have to stop this, right? Like, I have to stop them, right?"

And I thought, *Oh my God. I'm thirty-five years old and embarrassing myself in my own house, with my partner, in front of her family.* I wasn't yet sure what to do with the realization. I kept drinking my five nightly beers for a little while after. But I did download *This Naked Mind* in audiobook.

Nothing too dramatic prompted me to finally listen to it. But during a week when I was getting drunk every night and waking up hungover every morning, when I'd humiliated myself in front of my partner's family, something in me finally decided, *Let's give that book a listen.* I was washing dishes while I listened to the introduction on my headphones, and I'll never forget the relief that started to wash over me as Annie spoke. I realized, *Oh my God, there's a way out of this.*

I immediately connected with Annie's story, the one where she talks about waking up at 3:33 every morning. I recognized myself—how I'd wake up, panic, drink more to get back to sleep. I decided the book was interesting, but that I'd keep drinking as I digested it, and that I wouldn't tell Mary anything about it. I didn't want to get her hopes up. I didn't want to make a big production out of an announcement I'd made so many times before—*I've figured it out! I know how to control my drinking!* Those promises were empty; they never amounted to anything.

A couple of days after I started listening to Annie's book, I was sitting in the kitchen with a beer in my hand, the heavy, hoppy taste sour on my tongue, and realized, *I'm done. I don't want this anymore.*

I could see the whole evening unraveling with that last sip—the crying, the heavy, sickly feeling of drunkenness creeping over me, the aching around my eye sockets the next morning. I saw the future. I saw the tunnel ahead. I thought, *Holy crap. I think I'm done with this forever.*

The next day, the same thing happened. I got out a beer and realized I didn't want it. I kept thinking about this passage from the book: "Alcohol does pick you up, but only from how far it kicked you down, never up to where you were before you started drinking."

And I thought, *I want to know what it feels like to be higher than this.* I loved my life. I was so happy. And I knew I didn't deserve to punish myself like that. I'd found a way off that train. I haven't had a drink since. I stopped and haven't looked back. It's been the most powerful, transformative experience of my life. I signed up for the thirty-day alcohol challenge. I'd already quit drinking by then, but I checked in every day because it felt like a family.

I was worried, though, that Mary and I would go out as a couple and I wouldn't be crazy, fun, drunk Wyatt anymore.

But Mary was noticing the change. At first, she didn't say anything. One night I only had two beers, and she told me she thought something was wrong. The next, I just had one, and she thought, *I wonder if Wyatt's just experimenting?* Then the next night, I didn't have a drink at all. She didn't know what to say, because she didn't want to jinx it or make me feel pressured. But now that she understands my process, she's thrilled. She says it's changed everything, that my sobriety has been a gift.

A few months later, Mary had a huge homecoming show in Seattle to celebrate her new album. Macklemore performed a song with her. It was an incredible night. I heard every note, the gorgeous nuances in every song. I saw how the crowd responded to the emotional resonance of every lyric. She said it was the best show she'd ever had. I thought so too. And I realized that for the first time, I was there. I was present.

We still go to bars, and Mary drinks in front of me—and it's just fine. I don't have to ask anyone else to change. It's just an activity I get to not do—like how I don't snowboard because I don't particularly like it.

My confidence has grown every single day since I quit drinking. I'm better at my job. I'm better in my relationship. I was on *Jeopardy!* I think sobriety is really just a start for me, the start of this much longer journey. I'm thirty-five, but I feel like I'm becoming a real grown-up and taking responsibility for myself, for what I've been through, for self-care. I've learned alcohol cannot and does not enhance my ability to deal with tragedy, stress, excitement, or anything else. It just dragged me down. But getting sober is like exercising all those muscles that make me stronger and better able to deal with whatever life throws my way. Not drinking gives me more energy, more faculties to do stuff and be better. There was a period of initial fog that I don't want to downplay, but now I wake up excited, asking, "What's going to be different today?"

As I embark on this, I'm so grateful for the platform I have. Mary's fans reach out to me on Instagram sometimes, asking for advice. They're so into her life, and I don't blame them. I'm looking forward to sharing this experience with them, giving any of her fans who need hope in this area insight into what all of this looks like. Maybe we can inspire that same kind of mindfulness. I really do think the most powerful part of this is modeling it, spreading the gospel of this being possible—because, for most of my life, I didn't think it was.

If the train you're on is going to a bad place, there's hope, I want to tell them. *There's a way off the train. And you can find it.*

"Thinking something is true often makes it so."
—Annie Grace, *This Naked Mind*

IF IT CAN HAPPEN TO ME
Raegan's Story

I had an ideal childhood growing up in Richmond, Virginia during the 1980s and '90s. I attended a private elementary school, had a close circle of friends, and was active in ballet and year-round swim team. Summers were spent at the local pool, attending Vacation Bible School, and basking in the southern sun while boating, fishing, and swimming at my family's cottage on the blue waters of the Chesapeake Bay.

It was as close to a perfect upbringing as one can get in this world, and I honestly wouldn't change it for anything. Above all, no one in my immediate family suffered from alcohol or drug abuse, and my innocent, young eyes rarely witnessed a person who was under the influence. I was completely shielded from that dark side of humanity.

At age thirteen, I was exposed to alcohol for the first time. School was closed due to snow. That afternoon, three neighborhood friends walked over to my house and asked me if I wanted to go for a walk with them. I grabbed my heavy winter coat, gloves, and hat and dashed out the door. Once we approached a field on the edge of some woods, we stopped walking. They pulled out wine and beer—enough for all four of us. I followed their example and took a sip of the beer. I honestly don't remember much other than I thought it tasted absolutely disgusting. I was amazed to see one of my friends chug her can as if it were a Diet Coke.

The experience was so unappealing that I didn't take another sip until college. You read that right—I didn't drink again until college. I went through my entire high school career without a drop of alcohol. And it wasn't like I was some outcast who didn't partake in the traditional high school experience. In fact, the opposite was true. In many ways, I was like millions of other American teens. My weekends were spent with friends, attending our high school football games, shopping at the mall to grab the latest fashion trends, hanging out at the movie theater, and spending countless hours on the phone discussing the latest *Friends* episode. Alcohol never played a role in my life during those years. Classmates and friends would occasionally sneak it (some more than others), but I was never pressured into drinking. I chose not to, and no one seemed to mind.

The same can be said about my college years, at least for the most part. I think I drank a total of ten times during that entire four-year period. I occasionally attended parties across campus and at friends' apartments throughout Virginia Beach, but I rarely consumed any alcohol. I certainly didn't experiment with any illegal drugs. I would bring a Diet Coke to parties, attending to simply enjoy time with friends and meet new people. I wasn't against drinking, and I didn't mind that many of my friends would stumble back to their dorm rooms under the influence (it was their choice, after all). Personally, I just never felt the need to drink.

When college ended, I immediately applied and was accepted to a graduate school that was also located in Virginia Beach. These would turn out to be some of the best years of my life.

I entered the program at age twenty-three and immediately formed amazing new friendships, while maintaining most of my old ones from college. During this two-year period, I studied abroad at Oxford University in England and traveled with friends to New York City, Mexico, and Russia (twice). I also started to work on my first book that would eventually be published and sold out due to popular demand. Most importantly, I completed my degree, earning an MA in public policy.

I started drinking more but not to the point that it interfered with my life. Sunday through Thursday was dedicated strictly to school and work. However, I let loose and relaxed on my Fridays and Saturdays. I had a close circle of friends, and every Friday and Saturday night was spent playing volleyball followed by hanging out at someone's apartment or house, drinking our favorite alcoholic beverages while playing card games, building bonfires, and relishing our time together as carefree twenty-somethings.

During this time, I "discovered" mixed drinks. Prior to that, I'd only tasted beer and wine coolers, not enjoying either. However, when I was introduced to rum and Coke, vodka and cranberry, and a host of other beverages, I started to develop a taste for alcohol. Still, it never once interfered with school or work, so I didn't think I was doing anything wrong. Not to mention alcohol is legal, which sent me the message that everything was OK. Little did I know I was building a tolerance to a toxic poison.

By the time I completed my graduate program, I was all of twenty-five years old and ready to take on the world. I entered politics and started working in Washington, DC. My office had a perfect view of the city, yet I was still so young and naïve. I had stars in my eyes every time I walked by the US Capitol or the White House. It was the equivalent of a young actor arriving in Hollywood.

My weekend drinking with friends slowly turned into weeknight drinking with coworkers at happy hours or political events. Yet, it still wasn't an issue. It wasn't interfering with my job during the day, and it wasn't out of the norm for everyone I worked with (whether in the office or around the political scene in the city) to wine and dine at the strike of 5:00 p.m. and last for three to four hours. I never felt particularly pressured to drink with them—I just participated because I thought that's what a person in politics did after hours. I was following their example, and since alcohol is a legal substance, I never imagined these seemingly innocent afterwork drinking episodes would lead down a destructive path.

Five years later, I moved out to California to attempt to earn my PhD. While the degree ended up eluding me, I spent three years in the Golden State. For the first time in my life, I had more free time for meeting and dating new and interesting men. It was exciting but nerve-racking at the same time.

My roommate suggested I have a drink before each date, claiming that the alcohol would take the edge off, making me less nervous. I took her advice, and soon I was drinking not only to relax but to fall asleep at night. It wasn't long before I was relying on alcohol for almost every situation, considering it my "go-to" thing for any emotion. If I was happy, I drank. When I was sad, I drank. If I was celebrating an accomplishment, I drank. It became a part of my daily routine. Yet, it still didn't interfere with work, family, friends, or life. I didn't realize how out of control I really was.

I had no idea what was in store for me when I said goodbye to California after three years, but I headed back east. I planned to return to the political world; however, after one day in DC, I was attacked by a person I should have been able to trust.

This happened almost two years ago, and my drinking went from being something that occurred mostly at night to something I did no matter the time. It could be six o'clock in the morning, and I would easily down a can of beer or several shots of vodka. It didn't matter what I poured down my throat, so long as I passed out. That was my goal, to fade out of consciousness and to not think, not feel.

After about eight months, I entered a treatment program in another state that would include daily AA meetings. However, this did little to help me. When the three-month program ended,

I started another one to address the PTSD I'd developed after the attack. This program helped a great deal more than the first. My emotional needs were finally being treated, but I still went back to drinking on certain occasions—sporadically, but often enough.

When the trauma became overwhelming, I was still viewing alcohol as a "friend" to help me get through it. That all changed when I saw an online advertisement for the book *This Naked Mind* by Annie Grace. It claimed to have a different approach to alcohol—a more scientific one.

I ordered the book, started to read it, and as they say—the rest is history.

While I'm not taking a shot (no pun intended) at AA, it didn't help me. Thousands regain their sobriety through these meetings, and that's great, but it wasn't something that resonated with me personally. That's where *This Naked Mind* came in.

In the book, Annie Grace stated a fact that really clicked with me: "Willpower is not enough to control our drinking." Remember, alcohol kills hundreds of thousands of people all over the world every year. We often know we need to stop—I did. I just didn't know how. We need to recognize how alcohol impacts our brains and blurs the line between fact and fiction. We need to stop viewing it as something positive and realize the truth—that it is not only a drug but the deadliest drug out there. Just because it is legal in most parts of the world doesn't assuage its destructive potential.

Another glaring fact I learned while reading the book: our society has made us believe alcohol is something good, something we need to swallow in order to relax, to have confidence, to aid us when we're feeling down, to enhance our happiness when we're up. None of this is true! I will repeat, none of this is true!

Daily, we're bombarded by ads on TV and billboards. Ads that make us believe alcohol is our "go-to" for fun, finding the "right" partner, and unwinding when we've had a long day. These ads don't tell the truth—which is that alcohol will eventually steal from us. It takes our money, our happiness, our dignity, and even our friends and family.

Now, thanks to *This Naked Mind*, I see alcohol for the poison it is. I realize no one is immune to the horrors of drinking. I'm a perfect example of this. After all, I didn't grow up around alcohol. No one in my immediate family had a problem with it. I never drank in high school, rarely in college. But I wasn't safe from its clutches. It nearly took me down, seemingly out of the blue, when I hit my mid-thirties. If it can happen to me, it can happen to anyone.

I'm happy to say that today I can look at bottles of wine or cases of beer in the grocery store without even the slightest desire to add them to my shopping cart. I can go out to eat with friends, happily order a Diet Coke, and feel no need to ask for a shot of vodka to go with it.

To be honest, just the thought of consuming alcohol makes me feel ill. I'm rediscovering the person I was prior to alcohol's stranglehold on my life. I'm on the road back to becoming the successful writer, world traveler, dedicated friend, and positive, outgoing person I really am.

Alcohol has no place in my world, and I am more than happy to leave it where it belongs—in my past.

And I owe my sobriety to *This Naked Mind*. This book saved my life.

"You can find freedom, and it may be one of the most joyful experiences of your life."

—Annie Grace, *This Naked Mind*

HEALING MYSELF
Erin's Story

Life has always been hard. If you want, you can call me Negative Nancy, because what you're about to read isn't pretty. It's my story—the hard and the tragic and the devastating. But it's also the story of how I put the pieces back together into something beautiful.

My parents split when I was little, and every memory with my dad includes a drink in his hand and alcohol on his breath—still, to this day.

My mom was a good mom for a while, until she wasn't. She started drinking heavily and seemed to stop wanting to be a mom. She let my sister and me sip her wine (and take puffs of her weed and cigarettes)—I think it made her feel less bad about getting shit-faced. She was a mean drunk, but for some reason, only to me. She flirted with my middle-school boyfriends. She liked to make fun of me—in front of me—to her friends. My grandpa was a drunk, too—I always heard stories of him ending up in jail for drinking and driving, plowing the car into a fence, spending nights at the pub.

When I was thirteen, my sister (two years older than me) became bulimic and drank a lot. It was an awful combo, and our mom was MIA. *So* many nights I took care of my sister while she OD'd and did many other horrible things I can never forget.

My mom tried a few things: locking our fridge and cabinets (thinking this would help), putting her (and me) through counseling, and finally sending my sister away to a mental hospital. I was put in a private religious school and was active in youth group at church. I was a good kid but already so broken. Then my mom remarried, and things at home somehow got worse.

When I was sixteen years old, on Thanksgiving Day, my mom kicked me out of the house. I never went back. I'm sure you're thinking, *Oh, this must be where she went off the deep end!*

Nope, not yet. Strap in. It gets worse.

I was homeless for a while. Then I got jobs and my GED and made things work. I met a guy and thought life was going to start getting easier. This is when I was introduced to the disgusting sugary nectar known as Arbor Mist. I drank it a lot. Things happened in that relationship that flipped my world upside down—the things I experienced, as a child still, chipped away at the tiny bit of self-worth I had left.

I learned that drinking helped.

The relationship ended. I made a not-so-smart choice one night, and I got pregnant at eighteen. Best thing that happened to me. When I told the father, he vanished. My daughter is eighteen now, and I haven't seen or heard from him since that day. The good news is that I did stop drinking that shit wine when I got pregnant. Four months in, I learned that my baby had gastroschisis (her intestines were on the outside of her body), and life was about to get much harder. I was put on antidepressants and asked if I wanted to terminate. Obviously, it was a big *no* from me.

As you can imagine, I was high-risk and watched closely from that point. One month before her due date, her intestines almost ruptured, and it was time for an emergency C-section. She was rushed to her first operation and spent one month in the NICU. She had two more operations in her first three months of life. By the way, I'm nineteen at this point in the story.

Eighteen months later, I met the man who became my first ex-husband. He was abusive in all the ways. So, why not have another child? My son was a big, healthy baby (he now has severe allergies and some other special needs), and being a mom was the only thing I loved.

The marriage didn't last long. After months and months of mental and verbal abuse, rape, and my body shutting down on me, I escaped with my children.

Here's where I really started drinking (my early-to-mid-twenties). I was exhausted. As Annie Grace says, "Alcohol erases a bit of you every time you drink it. It can even erase entire nights." That was my goal. I had already spent so much of my life feeling not good enough, unwanted, damaged, uncertain of my identity, hypervigilant, and anxious. Um, *yeah*, I wanted to erase it.

Life was hard, and wine made it go away.

I started being really stupid. I got trashed on business trips and don't remember how I got to my hotel room. I drove drunk. I blacked out. I managed to quit drinking twice for about a year each time, cold turkey. But those attempts at quitting weren't for *me*, or because I really thought I had a problem, but because of not one but *three* successive alcoholic boyfriends, with whom I attended AA or Al-Anon or therapy.

The last time I started drinking again, I was able to stick to no more than two glasses at a time, but this was every day. I was oddly OK with this. I felt like I was in control, so there was no problem. I passed out on the couch many nights, spilling the glass in my hand, which strangely was usually a third or fourth glass . . . how'd that happen?

Then I met my soon-to-be second ex-husband. Everything we did involved alcohol. It felt fun and magical, and our friends' lives revolved around alcohol, too, so it didn't seem wrong or bad in any way. I remember *so* clearly the night I thought, *Damn, he drinks a lot.* We *drink a lot! Eh, it's fine.* And it progressed from there. I noticed a lot of red flags—lies, other women—and washed away my concerns with more wine.

And then I needed more.

I got to the point of drinking a whole bottle of wine per night, plus cocktails if we went out, had friends over, or just wanted them. I knew I had a problem. I needed to quit. I didn't want to think about alcohol. I didn't want to feel like I needed it to fit in. I didn't know how to stop. So many mornings, I'd wake up feeling physically and mentally awful and tell myself, "I'll do better today, today I stop," and then by 4:00 p.m., I was ready to drink again.

Shame and guilt ate at me every day. I started having health issues—palpitations that landed me in the ER and at a cardiologist. It was "just anxiety." I had a breast cancer scare and liver and skin issues, and my stomach was always a wreck. I drank more to get the palpitations to stop. I'd avoid meds at the dentist so I could drink that day. I had surgery and drank heavily the same day. I blacked out and apparently put on an extremely embarrassing performance for my kids and ex, which I have no memory of. I drove drunk. I can't remember a lot of nights.

How am I still alive?

I knew I needed out . . . of the drinking and the marriage. I was working on myself daily, until I was a few glasses in. Repeat. One day I was searching online for help, again.

I searched, *How to actually quit and make it stick and stop feeling shame and failing.*

The first article I read mentioned Annie's work, then another, then another.

OK, OK, I get it, I'll get the damn book!

I downloaded it on Audible and started it the next day on my way to work at a job I hated. I couldn't stop listening! I finished it *so* quickly—I couldn't get enough! Learning about the physical effects of the poison I was putting in my body, how so many other people have gone through this same struggle, and how to think a few steps ahead—asking myself questions like, *How am I going to feel in the morning if I drink tonight?*—it clicked!

I had my day one. I got an app to track it. I joined a FB group. I started following Annie on social media. I was *in*. Then day five. Then ten. It was hard, but I was doing it!

My husband still drank, which made it harder. I thought about wine all the time, but I was so proud of myself and that felt *so* much better than the shame!

I quit my awful job, started my own business, and started creating the life that *I* wanted for once—following my desires and passions, focusing on what made me happy! I went slowly, healing my traumas, working through my shit, being a good mama, and making sure this was going to stick before doing anything too drastic.

I left the toxic relationship 129 days ago, and I've worked on healing myself in *all* the ways every day since. I just celebrated nine months of being alcohol-free. I stopped taking antidepressants one week ago. I'm healing my body and my mind and doing things I love, and I'm truly happy. I drink mocktails from fancy glasses every day, and I never want to drink alcohol again!

For the first time *ever*, I love myself. My eyes well up writing this, but I wouldn't be in this amazing place if it weren't for Annie and her work. My life has changed in so many ways, and it's crazy that it all started with a book that I found in a Pinterest post.

"We are not weak; we are strong. We represent the very pinnacle of existence, stronger and more capable than anything we know of. We populated and explored the entire planet and even the moon before most of our modern medical discoveries."

—Annie Grace, *This Naked Mind*

UNTIL IT WASN'T
Becca's Story

I can remember the very first time I drank alcohol. I remember the feeling. I remember the place. I remember knowing that I really liked the way it made me feel.

I was twelve.

My mom had told us over and over that alcohol was bad and that addiction ran in the family—that we should always turn down alcohol if it was offered. What I didn't know was that my dad was an alcoholic, and my parents' divorce—two years before my first sip—was because of it.

After that first experience, I didn't drink until high school. Even then, I'd drink hard for a while, party a good bit, and then try to be "straitlaced." But I was always a little bit of a rebel, a learn-the-hard-way type of person. In college, I nailed down my routine: Party Wednesday through Sunday at a different venue every night. Take off Monday and Tuesday to reset. Start over.

Then I met my future husband at a nightclub when I was twenty-one. I knew immediately that he was a good man and that I was going to marry him. And I did—within six months of meeting him! Once we married, I slowed down drastically and didn't drink for about ten years. I had four kids very quickly—what can I say, we didn't have a TV—and was either pregnant or nursing for five years straight. That made it easy. To be honest, I really didn't even think about drinking during those years. It was a nonissue. I had more important things that needed my attention.

I don't know exactly when alcohol again became a bigger presence in my life. It happened slowly. At first, it was just for fun. My husband and I drank when we were out of town but never at home with the kids. I'd have some wine on girls' nights out, which my husband supported in the beginning because it was a way for me to let go and relax.

It was fun, until it wasn't. Everything about it was fun, until it wasn't. Sex was better, until it wasn't. Vacations were more enjoyable, until they weren't. Falling asleep was easier, until it wasn't. Relaxing was a given, until it wasn't.

You get the point.

Alcohol stole my ability to enjoy the good things in life, until I started manipulating my life to allow myself opportunities to drink.

The idea of a "rock bottom" was always in the back of my mind. *I haven't hit rock bottom*, I would think. *I have a job. I'm a successful Pilates trainer. I have four kids. I don't pass out at night. I don't post ridiculous stuff on social media. I must still be in control.*

It wasn't until I happened on *This Naked Mind* that I knew it was OK to question my drinking. For the very first time, I had permission. There was nothing wrong with me, I learned as I read. I was on the normal track—alcohol is designed to be insidious and addictive.

When I say I don't remember exactly when alcohol started taking up more energy than it was giving, I mean it. However, I do remember the exact moment I knew enough was enough, as clearly as I remember my first drink in middle school.

I was fat, I was tired, and I wanted off the alcohol roller coaster.

It was June when I bought *This Naked Mind*. I started reading it and decided that on September 1—my birthday—I was going to start a thirty-day break. But I didn't tell anyone, not even my husband. He knew I wanted to lose weight but not that I was struggling with alcohol. We had a beach trip planned for September, and tradition won out—I drank a lot on the beach. The break ended up lasting twenty-two days.

That was enough, I decided. It'd been fairly easy. I hadn't struggled through it. I reasoned that meant I was in control of it.

Then came the evening on the porch watching the sunset, the evening I remember most of all. My husband realized I'd been sneaking drinks when he wasn't around, hiding my alcohol use from him. I tried to lie, but he knew I'd been doing this for a while, even though he'd never asked me to cut back and I'd never told him I wanted to.

I had no explanation for why I'd been hiding it. That moment of having to come face-to-face with the truth of what I'd been doing was one of the most trust-breaking moments of my married life. I had a very strong marriage, but I realized that night that I'd been having an affair—not with another man, but with alcohol. It had become bigger than my love for myself, my husband, and my family.

Looking back, I was afraid to admit how much pain I was in. I was supposed to be strong. I was supposed to be superwoman. I was supposed to be supermom. I'd overcome so many challenges in my life, and I thought I had it together. But I was hurting and didn't even know it.

I finished reading the book and bought a ticket to attend the live event. A week or so later, I put up the bottle for good and haven't looked back.

Many, many stories brought me to that point in my life—stories of sneaking wine, of embarrassing evenings, of nights I don't even remember, of disappointing my family, of promises I broke over and over again, of missing days of work, of purposelessness and shame. Those are stories for another time and place.

What I can tell you is that my life looks completely different now. I never knew life could be this rich. I feel alive! I am thriving in this thing called life! My husband and I have purchased the Pilates studio I helped start eleven years ago. My children—even though they're adults—have a fully present mom back. I've helped other people radically change their lives for the better.

All because one person wrote a book and I happened to read it. All because *This Naked Mind* gave me permission to question my relationship with alcohol before I hit rock bottom. All because I learned there was nothing wrong with me but everything wrong with the substance I was consuming.

I am forever grateful!

"Once I was honest about my drinking, suddenly others felt like it was OK to question their drinking, too."

—Annie Grace, *The Alcohol Experiment*

HOW TO FALL IN LOVE AGAIN
Ryan and Alison's Story

Ryan

Monday morning, October 8. Ali wakes me up around ten in the morning, calling my name from upstairs. I roll over. My eye hurts. Stumbling groggily to the bathroom, I take in my reflection in the mirror. A large, bloody gash stretches across my face. My eye is black and swollen shut. I was supposed to be at work three hours ago.

What happened? Why is my eye like this? I try to think in reverse.

Rewind.

A weekend-long binge. A Sunday night fight. All the drinks. Staying up late. The trashed room. That fight . . . was the worst one ever. Did the kids hear all that? What happened to my face? Did . . . Ali hit me? What happened to my life?

Three weeks prior, Pearl Jam tickets! Ali goes drink for drink with me at the bar before the show. We leave early, after she throws up all the booze on the floor. But I'm not mad. I'm just happy to get home and do my nightly routine of drinks and cigars in the yard.

A few weeks before that, Ali is pulled over by the police and somehow passes a sobriety test even though she blows a 1.1 after the fact. I'm too drunk to pick her up.

Months earlier, the health problems are catching up with me. Swollen ankles, swollen pride, falls. I'm dizzy just trying to cross the street—turns out it's the drop in blood sugar.

Years ago, I realize I drink too much. But how can I change? *This* is just who I am.

After my doctor gives me a lecture about my blood pressure, I see *This Naked Mind* on Facebook. I buy a copy and read it cover to cover. Amazing information! A whole new approach. It strikes me as a way more doable alternative to the AA program my mom swears by. I decide to try a month without booze. I pick February because it's the shortest month. After two weeks, I'm so proud of myself that I decide to celebrate with a drink. I don't remember anything else about that night, though I can confirm the hangover the next day. I decide I'm destined for a drunken life.

I'm drunk when Ali tells me we're pregnant with our second baby. Alcohol ruins that memory for both of us. I can't remember, and she'd rather not.

I start drinking in my twenties as a crutch to deal with my depression and anxiety. I never plan for alcohol to take over my mind and soul, but it sucks me in deeper and deeper until I don't recognize myself anymore.

As a teen, I don't touch alcohol at all—I'm afraid of it. I see my mom's struggles and don't want to live that way.

Fast-forward.

One thing is clear on that October morning as I stare at my bloodied face in the mirror: I've truly lost control of my drinking. But Ali and I were both drinking, so it can't *all* be my fault, right? I lean my head against the mirror. It doesn't matter whose fault it is. Something has to change or I'm going to die—or worse.

Alison

I remember the days leading up to the worst night of our lives. Ryan had a weekend full of parties to go to—"kid parties," ostensibly, that were still full of adult beverages. I played tennis pretty badly because I'd had too much to drink. Then I went to a concert, drank some more, came home . . . and we had the worst fight of our lives.

I don't even remember what was said. The memories I do have are fragmented—picking up pieces of glass, wondering why the piano had been moved, asking what picture frames had been shattered, feeling guilty that the kids could hear the whole thing. Finally, we went to bed.

I woke up hungover, moving slowly as I got ready for work. Our youngest came in the bedroom and asked, "Why's Dad on the couch with blood on his hands and face?"

I thought she was joking.

By the time I got downstairs, Ryan was already in the bathroom, staring at his bloody eye in the mirror. It looked like someone had beaten him up or he'd gotten in a car accident.

My body felt numb. *Did I hit him? We fought, but I . . . wouldn't do that.*

Then I remembered that we'd made up and gone to bed. His face hadn't been bloody then. I'd remember if it had.

"Did you drive somewhere after I went to bed?" I asked. "Did you get mugged? Wreck your car? What happened last night?"

He said he'd gone to the nearest store to buy cigarettes. Maybe he'd hit something and the airbag went off. I ran out to check the car, but it was in pristine condition, parked normally in the driveway.

Ryan thought about it more and said he remembered parking the car and then being back home and pouring another drink at five in the morning.

Ryan

It takes a couple of days to piece together what really happened—I passed out behind the shed and landed on the ground sometime before five, smashing my face on a piece of wood and bleeding all over the cobblestone. Nobody sets out with that in mind while mixing a drink.

That morning, I cry a lot. I tell Ali I've hit rock bottom and that I wish I'd died out in the yard. We dump every drop of alcohol in the house, and I call in sick for the week to detox. Throughout the next few days, we have lots of honest conversations with our kids about what we're going through. We also pull *This Naked Mind* down from the bookshelf and take turns reading it again. After everything I've been through, I'm finally ready to take its message to heart for good. The book yanks back the curtain for us, helping us see the truth about booze and life and addiction.

Alison

Ryan committed to never drinking again, even though he still had alcohol in his system. I committed to not drinking . . . for a while. We spent the week trying to piece together what had happened that night, talking through what sobriety meant and trying to figure out how we might manage it, explaining to the kids what we'd done and what we hoped the future would look like. We avoided parties and people and embraced ice cream and books and genuine conversation with each other.

One of those books was *This Naked Mind*.

I was blown away.

How could this other life—this sober life—have been right in front of our eyes, and we'd never seen it? We read the book a few times, passing it back and forth, sharing memories—good and bad.

I kept telling myself I'd stay sober for Ryan. But three weeks in, I pieced together my own history.

I'd spent eight years in my twenties bulimic and anorexic and many years numbing my pain with alcohol—blackout-style alcohol, social alcohol, moderate alcohol, binge drinking alcohol—you name it, I covered it. I'd spent time pretending to be a tennis instructor, trying to hide my hangovers and lack of motivation. I'd gotten pulled over drunk, narrowly avoiding a DUI. Ryan was too intoxicated to pick me up.

It was never just one drink . . . always two, or three, or four, until I got that look in my eyes where I wanted to fight over nothing, or cry over everything, or just die. My battle with alcohol was the same battle I'd had with anorexia and bulimia. I couldn't just drink a little here and there any more than I could just throw up my food on occasion. As much as I wanted the answer to my insecurities and self-doubt to be as simple as tossing back a drink, I knew all my addictions would lead me down the same dangerous path.

And what I craved would never be found at the bottom of the empty glass.

Ryan

Weeks turn into months. We make it through the holidays completely sober. We learn how to lean on each other, and we learn how to fall in love again. But there's still a scar on my face to remind me of where we've been.

I now realize that I hadn't *lost* control of my drinking—booze had controlled me from day one. And though, on that terrible day, I thought I'd hit rock bottom, I now recognize how much further I could have fallen. I could have lost my wife, my kids, my job. I'm so grateful we steered the ship to safer waters before any of that happened.

We feel like new people, and I'm taking back my life. I no longer have the shakes or get dizzy during the day. My mind is sharper, my blood pressure and weight are lower, and my pride and dignity are slowly returning. I can make it through anything without a drink because I know the truth about alcohol. I don't envy drinkers, even when they're imbibing in front of me. Instead, I wonder which ones are fighting a secret battle.

These days, we're practicing meditation, breaking out our mountain bikes, and going on more walks with our dog. With each sober milestone, I feel the empty void inside me closing just a little more. I can see a time coming when I don't count the days anymore. I've made the transition from "not drinking" to "non-drinker," and it has filled me with more pride and strength than I'd ever felt possible.

It feels good to be alive—truly alive!

Alison

At first, I convinced myself sobriety was for Ryan, but really, it was for both of us. Reading *This Naked Mind* was the first time I realized I wasn't alone, that alcohol is a poison for us. That there's a better life out there for the taking.

Everything in my life is better since sobriety—our love for each other, our relationships with the kids, our enjoyment of each day. My husband and I have saved each other in more ways than I can explain. Our lives aren't perfect, and we still have stress, but it's easier to handle sober. I'm thankful every day.

I realize now that I kept trying to find myself with a glass or two or three of alcohol. I figured it would give me the courage I lacked, help me be centered and grounded and confident. Instead, it gave me courage to be someone I'm not, heightened my rage, handed me a one-way, nonstop ticket to bad behavior. It brought out all of the qualities I don't like in myself.

I am more centered and grounded than I have ever been. I feel more connected to my family, my friends, myself. This path we've chosen is something I'm proud to share with anyone who will listen so that others can be awakened into a whole new existence. As Coco Chanel said, "Beauty begins the moment you decide to be yourself."

"Take baby steps and be gentle with yourself. . . . The beautiful thing is that once you tackle this cornerstone habit and reduce or eliminate your alcohol intake, you'll begin to implement a whole host of other habits almost by default. . . . I didn't know it at the time, but making that big change caused a positive ripple effect across so many aspects of my life."

—Annie Grace, *The Alcohol Experiment*

TAKING A BREAK
Pamela's Story

"Repetition" is one of my favorite words.

I'm an artist, a yogi, and a yoga instructor. For me, repetition is a magical approach to discovery and development. In art and in yoga, you practice and improve. You prepare and accomplish. You commit and go beyond the limitations you've always placed on yourself.

On the yoga mat, I physically feel shifts of empowerment in my body, but that hasn't always translated to my daily life. Why? Because our underlying beliefs take time to change. It requires effort to challenge the stories we believe are true, that have become ingrained in our subconscious.

For me, one of those stories is about the way I used alcohol.

Getting to the place where alcohol was small and irrelevant wasn't easy for me. I had years of repetition to unlearn, to redefine. But alongside those years of drinking, I had a parallel narrative—stories of the breaks I took from alcohol, and of what those breaks gave me.

The first time I cut alcohol out of my life, I was in my second year of art school and about to leave for a summer-long study abroad in France. I'd been "assessed" by a counselor. She determined I was not drinking to drink; I was drinking to get drunk.

My reaction was simple: Who drinks to drink? Tell me something I don't know.

Before I left for France, she had me sign an agreement. I wouldn't drink the entire summer. If I did, I'd have to go to AA when I got home.

Not fair! But I agreed. And I didn't have one cocktail or glass of wine the entire summer. No way was my free-spirited, art-student self going to AA. I'd been to one meeting, and that energy wasn't for me.

Steering clear of alcohol all summer wasn't easy, but do you know what I remember most? I accomplished more that summer than I did in an entire semester of normal school. Without the buzz, without the numbing effect of wine, I was vibrantly alive and prolific in my creative processes. My drawing skills became an extension of myself like never before. It wasn't just that I did *more* work—it was really good work. I was proud. I was confident. I was empowered.

When the summer ended and I went back to "real life," I allowed myself to indulge again.

The next time I took a break, I was in graduate school. About three or four months before my graduate thesis art show, I decided to stop drinking, remembering the art I produced during that summer in France. *This is what I came for. I'm here to do this as best as I can, which means no booze until it's done.* My desire for success outweighed my desire for alcohol.

Envision the art, complete the art, design the show, finish the paper.

It was another profound period of time. I again experienced that focus, clarity, and connection to the work. I was prolific and did some of my best art in years. I also shed fifteen pounds.

Then the show was over, and alcohol became part of what felt like normal life. I moved around the country for art jobs, then took a corporate role as a product manager so I could make enough money to start an artist residency program. During this period, I was earning more money than I ever had before, sourcing product at shows in Hong Kong, and setting up our booths in New York City, Chicago, Atlanta, and Vegas. No surprise, despite my binge drinking, I was a highly functioning professional. I showed up for work, even though I was sometimes more hungover than I would have liked.

I even got married to a wonderful man named Tom and became a devoted stepmom to his elementary-school son, Alex. My whole life was coming together. I had a family I adored, a good job, and a plan for the future.

Then the economy tanked, and I got laid off. For the first time since I was sixteen, I was unemployed. I was devastated and freaked out. But Tom was my rock—he still is. He called it "an open door." Where would I go next?

I decided to sign up for a five-month yoga teacher program. Power yoga is physically challenging, and I loved it. Part of me also hoped it would create a shift in my drinking habits. I wanted to be a "normal" drinker. As I progressed through the program, I became fitter and physically stronger. And it got *real* when it was time for our twenty-one-day cleanse. No dairy. No meat. No caffeine. No alcohol.

Much. Harder. Than. I. Thought.

But even though this third break was harder than the first two times I'd given up alcohol, I persevered. And I felt amazing. I had real hope that this was it—that I'd changed my relationship with alcohol and found my ability to moderate.

But over time, I found myself drinking at home in the evenings, imbibing while cooking, sipping cocktails on the weekends. And it wasn't moderate. It was becoming easier and easier to overdrink, to get messy and wake up ashamed, wondering what I'd said and done.

Maybe it's time for another cleanse, I decided. Tom and I planned our joint cleanse, but the day before we were scheduled to begin, we were struck by the greatest tragedy of our lives.

We lost our son. Alex was just thirteen.

Wine was my go-to numbing agent to tamp down the grief. But, of course, wine can't erase heartbreak. It only suspends it temporarily, provides a moment of hazy respite before the agony comes roaring back with a vengeance, along with the persistent urge for just a little more booze.

I had no idea how to cope with the emptiness. I signed up for a yearlong advanced yoga-teacher program in hopes it would bring me through to the other side, give me focus, help me somehow cope without drinking so damn much.

It didn't work. Day by day, month by month, I found the new equilibrium that exists on the far side of grief, but I didn't regain my vibrancy. As the years passed, drinking was my way of letting go—chilling out after a long day or week, an excuse to be festive and a little rowdy at neighborhood parties. I began to accept that this was just who I was, but the cycle was exhausting, and I was burdened by shame and regret.

Deep down, I flailed against it. I wanted to drink less, to drink less often, but I felt deprived at even the *thought* of taking a break.

But repetition is powerful. I'd taken breaks before—three times. And I'd felt like an empowered badass each time.

As I began to consider a holistic detox, I found *This Naked Mind*. It made so much sense to me, and I gave up my daily drinking habit. My first year was not one hundred percent alcohol-free—remember, I need repetition to really ground a habit—but each time I chose to drink, I used it as a data point. Those data points were the evidence that I did not need or want alcohol.

I still tear up realizing how much time I feel like I wasted not being fully present. I didn't have daily hangovers, but I hadn't even noticed how cloudy and numbed I was for too many years. Now, I have so much clarity.

My yoga practice comes from the inside out. I'm teaching with a clear mind and vibrant passion. I feel alive, honest, and available to my students, instead of feeling like I'm a hypocrite. My creativity is flourishing. I'm building and launching a new business. I'm writing. My art feels good—and it's selling! I'm empowered, and I feel awesome physically.

I had no idea life could be this way. I just wish I'd put the pieces together sooner.

The advice I give to people who are thinking about going alcohol-free is this: try out a break and see how you feel. The most important part is that you choose to do it from a place of curiosity and big, bold badass-ness. This is not about deprivation. It's about empowerment. I believe you'll love the way you feel. I think you'll be thrilled about your more radiant skin, better sleep, weight loss, and clearer thinking.

People will notice. Your loved ones will notice. You will notice.

I know the power of taking a break. I also know how easy it is to stay stuck in our habits. For me, choosing to live alcohol-free every day is the single best thing I have ever done for myself.

"Loving yourself includes getting to know yourself, accepting yourself, and making a conscious decision not to take your health for granted. You are the person you will be spending the most time with for the rest of your life, so stop judging yourself and take a minute to appreciate the true, miraculous nature of this body and mind that you've been given."

—Annie Grace, *The Alcohol Experiment*

THE POWER OF A SCIENCE-BASED APPROACH
Hannah's Story

College. Supposed to be the best years of our lives, right? Well, for me, it was when my drinking escalated and started creating problems. I'd started drinking toward the end of high school, and when I got to college, I was ready to party. College was a roller-coaster ride of bad relationships, blackouts, and way too many hangovers. Despite concern from my friends, I never felt like I could quit alcohol. I was in a sorority, and every social gathering revolved around taking shots or playing beer pong. There didn't seem to be a feasible way to be sober and still have a social life.

After I graduated, I made a conscious effort to cut down on drinking. I also began a healthy relationship with my current boyfriend. We drank together, but he never had more than two or three beers—I had to work hard to moderate to that level with him. I planned activities that didn't involve drinking and took weeks or months at a time off of alcohol. After about a year of this, I felt satisfied. I'd taken "control" over my drinking. Whatever problems I had in college had been eradicated by maturity, a serious boyfriend, and a full-time job. I decided it was safe to begin drinking "the way I wanted" again.

For a while, it seemed like it was working, and I was under

the illusion that I could drink safely and responsibly. Only on the weekends. Starting late at night. The warning signs were there, of course. I still had the occasional blackout at a bar, and once in a while I got too drunk and fought with my boyfriend. Beneath the surface, I had the vague sense that maybe my alcohol problems *weren't* completely gone. This made me uncomfortable. I shoved the thoughts aside.

My boyfriend and I moved across the country so he could go to grad school. It was an exciting time, but it's hard to make friends in a new city, and my job proved demanding. I found it easy to deal with my stress and loneliness by turning to wine at the end of the day. Before I knew it, I was drinking a bottle of wine a night, alone, three to four times a week. Soon, I found that one bottle didn't "do the trick" and started making several cocktails before I opened the bottle.

Four months later, I was miserable. My whole week had turned into a series of drinking binges and hangovers, and I wasn't productive at all at work. I struggled to get through each day, always looking forward to the wine that awaited me when I got home. Sometimes I'd wake up so sick that I needed a mimosa to get out of bed. This turned into a whole day of drinking, and the cycle started over.

This wasn't sustainable, and I knew it. I tried sticking to a three-drink limit when I went out, but it was impossible. I couldn't leave a bottle of wine unfinished. If I only had a couple of drinks, I would feel irritable and itchy, wishing I could have more. I never felt satisfied with a few drinks—it only made me want another one. The more I tried to control my drinking, the worse it got, and I was back to drinking at the dangerous levels I had in college. One afternoon, I found myself curled up in bed in tears, knowing that I was completely out of control. I only had one option: get sober.

As you can imagine, when I first tried sobriety, I struggled. I attended a twelve-step program and didn't resonate with the concept of a higher power. I also realized how uncomfortable I felt socializing sober and that I felt insecure and lonely without alcohol in my system. I fought and struggled for a year, and then I gave in. And it was bad.

It took that final binge to find *This Naked Mind*. If a twelve-step program didn't work for me and I had to get sober, I needed something new. I was fascinated—enthralled, really—by the scientific approach of *This Naked Mind*. Finally, something that made sense, that I could embrace wholeheartedly. I became very involved in The Alcohol Experiment and the online community. Instead of being told to submit to a higher power and not ask questions, I could have real conversations about the brain, addiction, and the media. It was an energizing, fulfilling, empowering experience, so different than my haphazard struggles with quitting before. *This Naked Mind* has completely changed my views on drinking—I now see alcohol as an unnecessary poison that steals my joy. Furthermore, I've discovered how much fun sobriety can be and have come to enjoy being fully present in life.

If you haven't seen sobriety as an option, or if you've tried conventional methods and they just haven't worked for you, *you* are the reason I've shared my story here. Because I've been where you are, and I can attest that not only does a science-based approach to quitting work, it leads to so much joy and fulfillment. It's so much better than drinking ever was.

"When you see alcohol as your mortal enemy instead of your best friend, you will love going out and not drinking. It will give you pleasure. Instead of hiding in the shadows, you will dance on your enemy's grave."

—Annie Grace, *This Naked Mind*

THE DAY I COULDN'T GET DRUNK
Mike J.'s Story

I've probably written this over a thousand times in my mind, but here I go this time, for real. Those who have spent any amount of time with me in the last twenty years know that drinking has been an integral part of everything I've done. To end something that was such a deep part of my identity was no small feat.

Lots of people have asked me why I stopped. In most cases, I just shrugged it off, saying I needed a break, but it was more than that. It wasn't a "hitting rock bottom" situation like so many stories you hear about. Nothing really bad happened that forced me to get my stuff in order, but that didn't mean I was OK. My alcohol use was impacting my work life, my family, my body. Things got out of hand so gradually that I almost didn't recognize it.

I remember a doctor's visit a few years back. I was pre-diabetic and overweight. She knew my health was suffering. She asked me at what point in the day I began thinking about drinking. I figured people with drinking problems drank every day and started before lunch. This wasn't me. I was safe. My pattern felt normal to me. Most people in my circles would have agreed.

But once-a-week happy hours turned into daily stints at the bar. Four thirty turned into one thirty. Two beers turned into more than

I'm ready to detail in public. Safe to say it was all in the name of fun, being social, growing my business, brainstorming, blowing off steam, celebrating a win, or numbing a loss. I always had an excuse.

In time, I had to drink more and more to catch the same buzz. That's normal for most, and I wore this tolerance like a badge of honor.

Then one day, sitting on a barstool after a meeting, I couldn't get drunk, no matter how much I drank. It wasn't working. I felt overweight, ugly, tired, alone, and sad. That's when I decided, *I don't want this anymore.*

It still took me a few more weeks to work up the courage to stop.

Sometimes people are put into your life for a reason. I'm so grateful for Annie Grace, who wrote *This Naked Mind*. I'd been successful with drinking hiatuses before, but I always found myself anticipating the end—that moment of freedom when I could dive right back into heavy drinking. Reading the book helped me break down all the reasons I had for drinking—and I had many. By the end of the book, I recognized them for what they were—excuses to continue to indulge in an addictive substance that wasn't helping me.

Equipped with a fresh frame of mind and a new awareness, I set out to quit—and this time, something was different. This wasn't going to be a drinking hiatus that somehow fit in between my birthday, your birthday, major/minor holidays, vacations, good days at work, bad days at work, work trips, business meetings, friends visiting, fundraisers, weddings, and Tuesdays. I needed to relearn how to do all these things without alcohol.

The biggest misconception about stopping drinking is that it is a single decision made once. But in the first year, I had to choose sobriety over and over again. It seemed like I made the decision at least a million times.

I felt a lot of freedom in the first six months. Like a weight had been lifted. (Some people call this the *pink cloud*.) I especially felt this in situations where people were drinking around me. Some say they can't be around drinkers when seeking sobriety. For me, it felt liberating. I never realized the burden that I carried during my drinking. Like many other things, I was numb to it. What I'm talking about is the burden of how I was going to drive home, of convincing myself that I was OK, of feeling sick as I sobered up, of my words or behavior, of coming up with a creative story as to why I wasn't home when I should have been, of hanging around people and situations that were no longer serving me, and so many other things.

The next six months were harder. As the excitement around it faded, I was left with the version of myself that I had been numbing and escaping for so long. That was both awesome and incredibly scary. Drinking used to be my answer to the highest highs and the lowest lows. My desire to drink was the strongest during those really good times and really bad ones. But I'm so grateful for the opportunity I had to face my lowest lows as my true self, under my own power, without alcohol, even though it felt difficult during that period.

I don't know if this sounds dramatic to you. But I felt like I needed to share it because, from the outside, people look like they have it together. Like they don't have deep, dark spots. That's isolating. It makes us feel like we're somehow alone, uniquely flawed. But it's not true. Everyone has a pit; everyone suffers. Few look into the pit and deal with it.

Drinking sedated my worries—but that meant it kept me passive, so that I didn't deal with the parts of my life that needed to be fixed. I drank instead of going after the things I wanted. I spent a lot of time avoiding my problems, obliterating myself on a barstool instead of acting.

There is always more work to be done, but I have accomplished so much. In the first year, I lost forty-five pounds without going to the gym even once. I read over fifty books. I bought a new car—the Jeep I'd always wanted. I built a new segment of my business that directly helped over six hundred entrepreneurs while doubling my revenues. There were other things too: I've never driven my Jeep drunk. The clothes that used to be my "skinny clothes" are too big now. I wear a belt (because I have to), and my belly doesn't uncomfortably rub against it as I walk or sit down. I don't wake up in the middle of the night thirsty. My kids can sip from my cup without asking what's in it. My wife likes me a lot more. I'm seeing more of the cool and funny things my kids do. I know who my friends are. I've dabbled in new hobbies and rekindled old ones. I've explored spirituality where I previously outright rejected it. I cured myself of a chronic ailment—though I'll spare you the details!

The day I passed the "two years of no drinking" mark, I was loading my mountain bike in my Jeep and laughed as I saw my yoga mat and climbing gear in the back.

Who is this outdoor hippie guy? I asked in wonder.

Past me—the me who drank—wouldn't recognize present me. But over those intervening years, I was able to design my lifestyle, to purposefully choose who I want to be without alcohol. Somewhere along the way—during the second year—alcohol became small and irrelevant. I don't think about it anymore. And in place of alcohol, I found a life I'm in love with that's only getting better. I love who I am today, and I owe that to Annie Grace and *This Naked Mind*. I'm so thankful, and I can't wait to see what's next.

"You cannot be brave without fear."

—Annie Grace, *This Naked Mind*

FEELING GROWN-UP
Nancy's Story

"Hey sweetheart, can you bring me a beer from the fridge?" my dad called from his recliner in the living room.

I collapsed to the ground with a dramatic sigh, my nine-year-old body going limp against the kitchen floor like a dead fish. "You make me do everything!"

The recliner groaned as he shifted his body weight. "How about a deal? I'll give you a taste of it."

My eyes shot open. Now *that* was an interesting bargain. I scooted up to my hands and knees and then stood, hopped to the fridge, and carried the beer very carefully out to my dad.

He ruffled my hair as he took the beer and popped open the can. "There's a good girl," he said. He handed it to me. "Careful. Use two hands."

I wrapped all ten of my fingers around the cold, metallic tin and pulled it up to my mouth, just like a soda. But it didn't taste like soda. The liquid was sour and a little gross.

I wrinkled my nose for the barest of moments. But then I forced a smile onto my face. It might not taste as good, but it felt very grown-up.

"You like that?" my dad asked.

I nodded, my face earnest and serious.

He reached for the beer and winked at me, then took a long slurp.

After that, it became almost like a game. Every time I brought him a beer, I got to take the first sip, and every time, I felt very grown-up and sophisticated.

Over the next few years, I looked with longing at the wine at Thanksgiving and the champagne at New Year's and longed to participate—not for the wine itself, but because it was a rite of passage in my household. I grew up in the '70s cocktail-party era, after all, and drinking was always a part of our family celebrations.

As I got older, my family started serving me full glasses of alcohol at holidays and special events, and when I became an adult, I structured my social life around drinking without even trying to. As an extrovert, I want and need to be around people. Most of my best friendships today were made over more than a few beers. I joined a church choir that went out drinking, played softball in a bar league, and became a regular at several local bars. Alcohol was intricately interwoven into my life.

As the years progressed, my drinking continued, and the many nights and weekends of bad, obnoxious, and unhealthy behavior escalated. I gained weight, made many bad decisions, threw up countless times, and got myself sick because of drinking. I cringe as I look back on it, but I didn't recognize it for what it was.

It only became obvious that something was wrong when I started seeing a nutritionist. As part of the treatment program, she asked me to write down everything I was eating and drinking.

Seeing it all there, in stark black-and-white on the page, I couldn't deny that something needed to change. I decided to cut back. For a little while, I succeeded. But once I broke my fast, the drinking began to escalate again—and then I found myself drinking more than I had before I started seeing the nutritionist!

The final straw in my struggle with alcohol was a trip to Ireland with friends that centered around drinking. I must have had one hundred pints of beer and numerous shots of whiskey over the course of six miserable days. I spent all of the time on the tour bus sick and hungover and the rest of the time drunk. As we boarded the plane to return home, my husband and I decided to dry out for a while. That trip was an eye-opener. Something was really, truly wrong.

But it's hard to go dry when so much of your life revolves around alcohol. Shocking, right? I could avoid alcohol by clutching at sobriety with clenched fingers and a tightened jaw, with anger and resentment and frustration and cravings. But it was still there, beckoning me back, reassuring me with its siren song that the whole world would look better if I just had a beer.

Then I found *This Naked Mind* in audiobook. I followed the instructions to listen a little at a time and let it sink in. Finally—something that resonated! Right away, I felt relieved and happy. Everything I heard made perfect sense to me. Of course I had trouble controlling alcohol!

Alcohol is physically and mentally addictive. The problem was never about me or my own lack of willpower—it was the alcohol itself and how the human body and brain are designed to respond to it.

For the first time in a long time, I felt hope when I thought about my relationship with alcohol. I'd finally found something that explained my struggles and gave me an answer for how to stop drinking—or at least cut back. I was excited to listen every day and move closer to taking control of my drinking. Since then, I've revisited the book in paperback, returning to it whenever I need extra help.

I used to spend my nights wondering how to stop drinking. Now, after so many years, I've found answers and hope. I'm not that little girl anymore, taking sips of beer and feeling grown-up. Instead, I'm finally able to move forward into the future with confidence and poise, interacting with others on my own terms instead of through the haze of alcohol.

And that, to me, feels truly grown-up and sophisticated.

"The great news is that you are not stuck. Your life can be complete and whole again without alcohol."

—Annie Grace, *This Naked Mind*

LIVING HONESTLY
Meagan's Story

She walked into our office in LA, and the casting director remarked on how good she looked.

She declared proudly, "It's because I stopped drinking alcohol!"

I was shocked, a bit horrified, and completely in awe of her decision. It was the first time I'd *ever* heard someone say they'd quit. I didn't understand how a person who looked completely normal could just . . . stop drinking. There was an authentic freedom and honesty in the way she expressed it that I've never forgotten. It came back to me often over the next few years.

When I started getting healthy and working out, my mom gave me *This Naked Mind*. I'd just moved to Paris to take a director-level role with the *New York Times*, and I wanted to be alert and focused. I finished the book my first week on the job, and right after, my boss took me to dinner with our other colleagues. With the book fresh in my mind, I ordered water.

My boss looked at me and asked, "You're not pregnant, are you?"

I was horrified. The last thing I wanted was for my new boss to think I'd just taken a very important job, for which they'd moved me to Paris, only to find out I was pregnant. I promptly ordered a glass of wine to prove I wasn't.

Yes, in hindsight, there were a lot of things wrong with that situation.

It was a perfect storm. I was already deathly afraid I was an imposter taking this job. I wanted to make sure I could fit in. And, as a people pleaser, I hated making others feel uncomfortable. No matter how much I wanted to quit drinking, I concluded, I couldn't turn down wine at dinner in Paris.

I'd started drinking at age twelve, with my babysitter. And my mom swigged martinis at home, so we'd just steal the alcohol from her liquor cabinet and replace it with water. She didn't notice.

My home life was volatile, and drinking helped numb the volatility. I got my first fake ID at age sixteen. Since I looked older, I could easily get into clubs with it. In high school, my friends and I would drive from Baltimore to DC and party until five in the morning, then we'd drive back drunk, and I'd make it to school on time.

It got worse in college. I'd brag about how I could party all night, go to class the next day, work a part-time job, hold down an internship, and star in a play, all while maintaining straight As and double-majoring. I didn't have a problem if I could do all that.

Getting roofied from the punch bowl at a frat party and waking facedown in my own vomit didn't stop me. Running my car into the side of a barricade on the highway and blowing two tires didn't stop me. Developing adult acne and a beer gut didn't stop me.

Thank God I never hurt anyone or got a DUI.

When I moved to England, drinking was even more accepted, and coworkers would often come in bragging about their hangovers. Finally, a place where I wouldn't be judged for drinking! But the drinking culture was different there. You could drink to get drunk on the weekends, but drinking during the week in small doses was suspect. My British husband really had that mindset, and he got so judgmental when I'd have a glass of wine with dinner on a weekday. For him, there was no point in moderation—you should either abstain or get drunk.

One day, I realized he and I had nothing to speak about without alcohol. Our relationship had been built on our social drinking lives. We split up. I drank more.

I loved alcohol, and I hated it. I had bouts where I'd go sober for a month or three, but during those times, I tended to lock myself away in my apartment. It made me feel more isolated, and I started associating sobriety with loneliness.

Then the fainting started. After a period of being alcohol-free, I'd have a drink and faint. I had a glass of wine on a plane and passed out while waiting for my Uber. Ended up with a concussion. Another time, I went to a concert after three months of not drinking. It was really hot, and I had a cocktail and fainted right in the bar. Then it happened again in Paris. This all took place within about a year and a half. My body was physically reacting to the alcohol. How many signs did I need?

After I left the *New York Times* to work in film, I had less and less of a routine. I'd have a shot of whiskey before leaving the house. I started drinking for fun during the day. Then the suicidal thoughts began. Here I was, living in Paris, my dream city, and working in my dream career, and I was thinking of killing myself? Something was terribly wrong.

On Christmas Day, a thirty-something-year-old friend got blackout drunk, and as I watched her, I realized I'd been surrounding myself with people who drank more than me to make me feel like I didn't have a problem. It woke me up. This *was* a problem. A serious one. I needed to find a solution. The next day, I joined an online group associated with *This Naked Mind* and decided drinking wasn't for me.

My people-pleasing self's biggest fear was that I didn't know how to date without alcohol. How do you break the ice without getting drunk? And would my friends still want to hang out with me?

I wish I could go back and reassure myself that I didn't need to worry. It's so interesting to me—I actually put on my online dating profile that I'm not drinking, so that I wouldn't feel like a freak when I just ordered water at dinner. But I've been amazed at how many people have gotten in touch and said, "Yeah, I'm not drinking either" or "I stopped drinking." It's opened up a whole new world of men who are interested in other things, who aren't trying to numb their emotions, with whom I can have riveting conversations.

And my friendships? Some of those have shifted, but in a really good way. It wasn't that my friends didn't want to hang out with me anymore—I just started realizing that some of my friends were really only fun when I was drinking. Those weren't deep, genuine relationships I needed to be investing my time in. I've let some of those ebb away, and I don't feel like I've lost anything. But my close friends? I've been amazed at how supportive they've been—in some ways, my choices inspire them.

For me, not drinking gives me a deep sense of freedom. It's what I've been looking for my whole life, and I had no idea that it was always there in front of me. I'm profoundly grateful for *This Naked Mind* and the peace it's given me.

I've been anxious for so much of my life. But I know now that I was always enough. Just showing up as myself was all that I needed. There was no reason to be anything other than my raw, true self. That in itself can inspire others. The world needs authenticity. A willingness to be vulnerable, to fight through the cognitive dissonance, and to live honestly makes us the warriors this world needs.

And now I can live like that each and every day.

"Drinking has become so prevalent, so pervasive in our culture, that it's difficult to escape its influence. But there's an amazingly vibrant minority of people who are taking a step back and thinking about that status quo. They've found they are participating in something that isn't much fun anymore, and they're choosing to pause and reflect. The result is an entire culture shift around alcohol."

—Annie Grace, *The Alcohol Experiment*

FINDING HEALING FROM C-PTSD
Terrance's Story

I started drinking later than a lot of my peers because my mom was a scary, unstable drunk and my brother was homeless from his addictions. I was afraid I would go down the same path if I started. The first time I drank, my freshman year of high school, I downed a handle of vodka at a party and woke up on a classmate's volleyball court covered in Taco Bell and vomit. And yet, somehow I knew that this was the beginning of a terrible romance.

I grew up poor—very poor. My mom and I lived in a shack among large homes in Napa, California. Ours was the house that none of my friends wanted to visit. I was relentlessly bullied because of how poor we were and how skinny I was. "You can't even afford to eat," they would say. I would leave the horror of school to go home to chaos, a sick mother, and my mom's revolving door of terrible boyfriends.

This is, of course, when I even went home. I would frequently stay at friends' houses for days or even longer. Often, I heard snarky comments from siblings and even parents, "Does he live here now?" or "Why doesn't he go home?" Their lives were always so much better than mine. They had a mother who wasn't a messy drunk; they had normal siblings who weren't living on the streets; they had a father they'd met. The polarization of "me" and "them" was very real to me, and the tracks that divided "them" from "me" were as loud as the train that rode them.

I was never comfortable in my own skin.

I drank a handful of times in high school, but it wasn't until college that I found myself falling for alcohol. That was when I first began treating what was becoming chronic and unmanageable anxiety.

I followed in my mother's footsteps and became a bartender. I'll never forget how great it was to know I could drink while working. I could calm the nerves and subdue my stress. It was a lot of fun, and for the first time ever, I was starting to feel like I'd found my place on this planet. Unfortunately, it was on both sides of the bar.

After I graduated from Sonoma State (first person in my family to ever go to college) and got a job with a small nonprofit in Sebastopol, California, my anxiety got more and more debilitating. I learned (on an unconscious level) how well alcohol seemed to work to relieve my suffering.

And then, it happened. I got a job at the hottest, most happening brewery in town! I was so excited! Now I could drink all of the time, and it would be normal. No—it would be awesome.

And it was awesome. Until it wasn't.

The culture at this place in Santa Rosa, California was very punk rock—drink fast and die young. Everyone was close, and we all drank together, all the time—even during our shifts. Especially during our shifts.

The establishment was always packed, and the job was as stressful and overstimulating as the money was good. I was cool for just having a job there, and I was *very* cool for drinking all the time. Which is what I did. My anxiety was out of control. But I just kept drinking and did all I could to subdue the distraught beast within. This was the first time in my life where I felt home. I had a family, and on the surface, they were just as fucked up and self-destructive as me.

This was also the first time I learned that if I just started drinking in the morning and kept it going all day, I could avoid the crippling hangover and accompanying anxiety that was waiting for me. I was at that job for three years, and eventually this unsustainable lifestyle caught up with me. I started missing work, and I knew my time there was limited. No longer was I falling for alcohol . . . now I was just free-falling.

I decided to move to San Francisco. I still worked at the brewery on weekends (because that's how good the money was), and during the week, I spent a lot of the time recovering from my weekend work/booze binges. On some level, I knew my drinking was getting worse, but I couldn't imagine not treating my anxiety with alcohol. What I decided was that I needed to get out of the bar industry. I quit the brewery (probably just before I would have been fired, anyway) and got a non-bar job in SF.

The non-bar job didn't last very long, and I ended up getting a bartending gig at . . . you guessed it! A very happening establishment. This time it was a college tequila bar, and once again, I was cool and surrounded by fellow heavy drinkers. Not surprisingly, by this point, my relationship with alcohol had become more tenuous. Blackouts were frequent, and awful hangovers turned into derailing benders. My tenure at this place lasted about two years and ended sourly.

At some point during my time in San Francisco, I had health insurance for the first time in my life. I regularly saw doctors for my unbearable anxiety. One doctor showed concern and began asking about my childhood. They connected me with a trauma specialist who diagnosed me with PTSD (complex PTSD, to be specific), and she said that the anxiety was due to a neurological response to the persistent trauma I experienced as a child. I needed to avoid alcohol. Little did she know, that ship had sailed long ago.

A few years later, I moved to Portland with my partner (whom I met in Guatemala), ready to experience the "beervana" that is Oregon. Weeks into our move, we found out we were pregnant.

I was still in the bar industry (again, a very happening brewery in Portland), and my partner—who was my partner in booze until she got pregnant—began to see how problematic my drinking was. Some terrible blackouts and my unpredictable and belligerent behavior had her very worried about the father of the child that would soon make its appearance. We decided to move to Eugene to be closer to my partner's family.

Something happened to my drinking in the first year of my daughter's life. I was working about sixty hours a week, and my partner was experiencing severe postpartum depression. And my drinking escalated to a whole new level. I would go on extended binges on a regular basis. I went to an intensive outpatient facility but still didn't take my sobriety seriously. Eventually, I stayed sober about nine months with the help of a Buddhist-centered recovery program. I didn't want to go to AA. I relapsed for six days, and I nearly lost everything. My life was in shambles, and I knew this time had to be different. So, I dove headfirst into AA. For the first time ever, I took my recovery very seriously.

Getting sober hasn't been all bunnies and rainbows. At about six months in, my anxiety was winning the battle, and I couldn't bear it anymore. In my head, I had two choices: I would drink, or I would kill myself. Drinking was no longer an option, and before I knew it, I was planning my own death. I just couldn't imagine living with the anxiety. Thankfully, I realized I had a third option—a Hail Mary appointment with my doctor, where I told him how serious it was. He put me on amitriptyline, and it changed my life. I no longer have anxiety.

Even though I got the anxiety under control, AA never felt like the right fit for me. Yet, for one year I "faked it till I made it," meeting some wonderful people in the process. Part of my daily program involved listening to podcasts. My favorite was *Recovery Elevator*, and one day, Annie Grace was a guest on the show. The things she said were groundbreaking. I told my partner about it, and she bought me *This Naked Mind* for my birthday. *This Naked Mind* (the book and the podcast) has been transformational for my mindset and my level of personal freedom and commitment to my new alcohol-free path.

I love how Annie Grace talks about alcohol overuse—that it's a trap that any drinker can fall into—and that she refutes the "alcoholic" model that divides people with a problem from people without a problem. *This Naked Mind* shines a light on this highly addictive drug instead of fixating on a supposed personal defect. The reality is that anyone can become addicted to alcohol. That knowledge mitigates the stigma around problem drinking. Instead of judging people, we can and must call this drug out for what it is: an addictive poison that is deeply ingrained in our culture. Alcohol is the only destructive drug we have to justify *not* doing.

This Naked Mind is the cultural shift we need.

My life today looks different than it did a year ago. I still attend AA but only one meeting—my wonderful home group that consists of many of my favorite people. Today, I listen to podcasts, I'm rereading *This Naked Mind*, I hang out with fellow non-drinkers, and I'm starting individual counseling. I'm so excited for this new chapter in my life—for what it means for my partner and me, for my daughter, and for the future.

"When I look back now, it's almost a joke how much happier I am without drinking! I can finally truly enjoy social occasions for what they are—a chance to hang out with my friends and have a good time. Whether they're drinking or not doesn't affect my own enjoyment. Only after alcohol has completely left your system can you fully realize that, yes, you can feel joy and happiness and incredible energy levels on a consistent basis."

—Annie Grace, *The Alcohol Experiment*

FULL CIRCLE
Kate's Story

I picked up drinking in my forties at the peak of a quintessential midlife crisis. The paint was peeling off my white-picket-fence life. Wine looked so promising on the heels of great disappointment. I'd just moved my family of eight across the country to answer "the call." I'd been steeped in Christian ministry and all things Jesus, and Kansas City was my "destination of destiny." I was headed to Bible school, a long-awaited answer to prayer.

That ended in four short months.

In the aftermath of losing that dream, I was forced to reckon with my unhappy marriage and my strained relationship with my dying parents. I'd been mourning the loss of my childhood for a lifetime, grappling with the legacy of my parents' alcoholism, and it snowballed into mourning the loss of the future I'd thought had been promised to me.

Grief lay like gauze on my arms, tangible, weighty.

Don't get me wrong—I loved being the overcommitted homeschool mom of six, because I was driven by a message that consumed me, one of healing for the brokenhearted and liberty for the captives. My heart broke for the marginalized, forgotten, rejected ones. I prayed that God would use me to help heal the hurting.

I just didn't know I was going to have to become one of them, first.

Kansas City was supposed to be my Promised Land, but it became the wilderness of my wandering. For more than a decade, I ran from my grief. I ran away from God, my husband, and the mission on my heart—losing it all at the bottom of an ocean of Red Zin.

Weekend drinks became daily drinks, a glass became a bottle, the wine turned into vodka. I never saw it coming—it just carried me away. I knew I was drinking too much, but I seriously believed it would go away as quickly as it came on.

But as it turned out, it wasn't a quick fix—it was a painful process. With much fear, I took myself to AA. What else was I to do? But I think the stigma and shame I felt just made it worse. The label "alcoholic" became my identity, changing how I perceived myself in every area of my life—on top of the grief and guilt, it became the perfect cocktail for disaster. I began sneaking my seedy little shots of vodka, which turned my struggle into what felt like full-blown insanity.

Sure, I was able to take breaks—two days, two weeks, two months—here and there. But I never lasted more than two months, and when I started up again, the shame came back thicker than ever. The drinking "events," as we call them, became exponentially more problematic. Alcohol took me to treatment centers, therapy, and even to jail. I've been escorted by ambulance to hospitals, by police back home, and by lawyers to court.

I'd become one of those desperately hurting souls I'd once wanted to reach.

Enter *This Naked Mind*.

A friend recommended it, and I read it while I was still drinking. As I learned more about the nature of alcohol, my jaw dropped! I felt so angry! Why hadn't anyone talked about this before? Where had this information been? I felt like I'd been lied to my whole life.

But I didn't quit drinking then, even though I wanted to. At my core, I didn't yet believe it was possible.

The next month, I did The Alcohol Experiment, and the month after that, I boarded a plane to attend a live This Naked Mind event, where I signed up for Annie's yearlong one-on-one coaching program. I was ready.

I was desperate.

For a time, it was still a battle. I found myself earning my second DUI a few months later, which was the catalyst for my very last binge.

But then I found my feet set on solid ground. With the faithful, consistent help of the coaching program, I found my brain rewiring. Shame fell away as I communicated my hopes and fears, successes and losses, and as I grew more confident in myself. I learned how to be uncomfortable, because there was so much hope surrounding me.

After so many years wandering in the wilderness, I'd found my Promised Land.

And the mission that had gone dormant within me began to wake up. Even before I'd totally walked away from alcohol, I knew someday I was going to help others get free, that this was my path to help heal the brokenhearted. It had been all along.

My journey was actually my destination.

I don't believe in accidents. Falling into drinking was the anvil that my destiny was hammered out on. Nothing is wasted, and I have profound gratitude that I've come through to the other side and stepped into my calling. I'm actually now certified as a This Naked Mind coach, and it is with fear and trembling that I walk forward to help others as I've been helped.

The message in me has come full circle. My broken heart is healed.

"Alcohol is addictive, and not only to some people—to all people."

—Annie Grace, *The Alcohol Experiment*

AFTER FORTY YEARS
Lesley's Story

Forty years. That's how long it took me to change my relationship with alcohol. That's why I'm telling my story—I've been inspired by hearing the journeys of others and the startling success of the *This Naked Mind* book and program. I want to add my voice to the mix in hopes that others will find freedom sooner than I did. In hopes that the next person won't take forty years to realize that alcohol is a real party pooper.

I started drinking socially around the age of twenty. Over the years, I had two children, and it seemed like my drinking was under control. I was a moderate drinker—isn't that what we all call ourselves? But things shifted bit by bit, life event by life event. Before I knew it, I'd tricked myself into believing that I could only really enjoy life with a glass of wine in my hand.

By my early forties, I loved wine. I drank when I was happy, when I was sad, when I was angry. I drank when I was anxious and when I wanted to celebrate—isn't getting off work every day a reason to celebrate? I was still managing my life—not very well—but I couldn't seem to get through a night without my faithful friend. And I was starting to notice that other people seemed to manage their drinking differently than I did. It was usually me instigating the social events or trips that gave us an excuse to drink. Yet, even while my life was coming apart like the loose pieces of a thousand-piece jigsaw puzzle, I still imagined myself as someone who had everything together.

Then my fifties hit. I'm not a big woman, and I was drinking a bottle or two of wine every night, from five until eleven. I was marinating in poison daily. The warning signs were there, and I started trying desperately to stop. But I couldn't. It had sucked me in. I was trapped.

About ten years ago, I went to an AA meeting. I hated every moment, but it did help me stop drinking for a time. A miracle! I stayed sober for fourteen months and decided I was cured. Surely I could start drinking again, just a little. In moderation. So I went back on the sauce. Before I knew it, I was back to a bottle or two a night. Sometimes I'd take a day off, but my health was wrecked. My memory was awful, my skin pasty, my eyes yellow. I knew—*knew*—my health was suffering, but I kept going. Cognitive dissonance in action!

It was still escalating. Eventually, I'd get in the car and drive to the liquor store at night to get more booze after finishing all the wine in the house. Once, I nearly ran into the median strip. Another time, I found myself on the wrong side of the road. Some mornings, I couldn't even remember going to the liquor store. It's absolutely terrifying to think of what could have happened.

One morning, I arrived late to a client's house with a dreadful hangover. I parked my car awkwardly and tripped over the front step. The client came to the door and said, "Oh, you're finally here."

I apologized for being late.

And then she asked the most horrifying question: "What have you been drinking this morning?"

I was gobsmacked. Shaking. I bolted into another room to prepare myself for work. Would I lose my job if she called the office? What had I done?

As I walked past the china cabinet, I noticed a framed plaque—the "Serenity Prayer." That's when I knew. The client was sober. I read the prayer over and over again. When I emerged from the living room, she had a serious expression on her face. She told me that she used to drink every night until she blacked out. Then she'd decided to give it up altogether. She'd gone to AA for a while but eventually stopped going and remained sober.

That's all. No judgment, no threats, no reminders that my behavior had been unprofessional. She just told me her story. I listened and thanked her for what she'd given me.

The next day, I drove to the waterfront and stared out at the sea. The cravings were coming at me in full force. I was desperate for a drink, but I knew I had to change what I was doing. I trudged back to the car, drove to a meeting, and sat in the back. For ninety days, I kept going to meetings and not a drop of alcohol passed my lips. Eventually, I stopped attending, but—like that client who gave me the profound gift of her story—I stayed sober. It's the online communities that have really helped me on my journey—especially the This Naked Mind community, which has been so inspirational. It gives me daily motivation to continue on my journey of sobriety.

Forty years. Each day I think back to those times when I was such a mess. I was barely functioning! And I wonder, *Why?* I don't truly understand what drove me to that dark place, but I'm so happy and free out in the light now. For the first time in decades. Now, I look to the future! What do I want to be when I grow up? Because we're all still growing.

See! It's never too late. If I can quit drinking, anyone can. And that includes you. I hope you won't wait forty years.

"When you stop believing you need to drink to have fun, you won't need to."

—Annie Grace, *This Naked Mind*

THE VERY WORST CHRISTMAS
Rob's Story

I never, ever thought my life would be better without alcohol. It wasn't just that I couldn't imagine going to a concert or a wedding without some shots in me; it was that I couldn't imagine a life without drinking in it, period. So when Annie Grace's smiling face suggested that my life could be better without alcohol, I didn't believe her.

But I did at least allow for the slim chance that she was right, because I had come to a point where I was desperate to grasp any straw that might get me out of the hole I'd dug for myself.

For most of my life, I was what you might call a "normal" drinker. I drank for fun, to have a good time, to mark special occasions, to socialize. Sure, there were many times I drank more than I should have. But in general, drinking wasn't a problem for me. I had "guardrails" that kept me in line: I never drank during the day. I drank mostly on weekends. If it got to be too much, something in me said, "Hey, slow down!" And I would.

But in recent years, I began drinking for more than just a good time. I drank because I felt anxious, scared, upset, whatever. I drank to avoid the sense that life wasn't turning out the way I'd hoped. I drank because I thought it made me a better person—more charming and alive, less inhibited and depressed. I drank because I thought it kept people from seeing the pain I was in.

With all that going on under the surface, I started to drink more. I started to drink daily. I started to drink more daily.

I knew I had a problem. I cast about for a solution. Within two years, I saw four substance-abuse specialists, tried meetings, and had intense conversations with friends and family. All the while my drinking increased. The embarrassing incidents, fights with my spouse, and hours wasted due to drunkenness began to add up. The blackouts, scary numbers from my doctor, and creeping realization that I needed a drink just to feel normal kept me running to the liquor store . . . you know . . . just to calm my nerves.

My bad times culminated a couple years ago in December. My daughter felt devastated over my drinking, and I'd promised her that when she came home for the holidays, I'd be sober.

And I was. I enjoyed five days of sober fun with her before she went to spend Christmas Eve with her mother. In her absence, I decided a bottle of champagne was in order. But there was no way I was gonna stop at one bottle.

When she returned the next day, she took one look at me and said, "You're drunk, this sucks," then went straight to her room and shut the door. Merry Christmas. The presents rested unopened beneath the tree. And things actually deteriorated from there.

Earlier that year, I'd stumbled upon *This Naked Mind* while searching for a book that would help me understand what alcohol was doing to my body. Reading Annie's book gave me hope, but I was still drinking. But the first Live Alcohol Experiment came along at the perfect time for me. A week after that awful Christmas—on January 1—I made a commitment to go alcohol-free. I haven't had a drink since.

I don't mean to make it sound easier than it was. The first two weeks were brutal. I approached those first thirty days of sobriety not with the intention of quitting for good, but rather of getting my alcohol problem under control so I could eventually go back to "normal" drinking. But I was still so shaky after the first thirty days that I felt I needed another thirty under my belt.

So, with the support of the great group of friends I'd made in The Alcohol Experiment, I re-upped my commitment. Thirty days turned into sixty. Sixty turned into a hundred, and a hundred into a year, and then some.

Indeed, Annie had been right. The fact that my life was *so* much better without alcohol made the decision not to drink an easy and obvious one.

Since going alcohol-free, I've achieved a level of emotional balance that I never thought possible. I am more confident, more productive, and more engaged in life than ever. Depression and anxiety rarely come into play anymore.

It's been the best time of my life, not because everything has gone as I'd hoped—far from it—but rather because I've become the best version of myself I've ever known. Sure, I still feel fear, sadness, anger—all the difficult emotions. But now I feel these things fully, without resistance, allowing these emotions to play the role in my life that they were meant to. I credit all of this to my usage of the strategies and tactics I was exposed to through *This Naked Mind*.

A while back, I wrote Annie a note. It said, "I don't know what it would be like to be a person who has had such a huge impact on the lives of others, and in some cases, maybe even saved people's lives. What I do know is that I'm one of your people, Annie, and as such I will carry you in my heart till I die. I'll never describe this remarkable transformation I've achieved without thinking of you."

"Your mind is incredibly powerful. It can be a staunch ally, or your worst enemy, depending on how you use it. The good news is that once you learn how the mind works, you can take control and use its power to change anything in your life."

—Annie Grace, *The Alcohol Experiment*

SORRY, I GOT DRUNK
Elizabeth's Story

Where do I begin?

Do I start at age thirteen, when I stole my first bottles of wine from the basement because I'd watched the adults around me seem to have so much fun drinking?

Or should I jump ahead to adulthood, when I was raped? Do I say that I was so drunk that I only remember bits and pieces, that I mostly remember the terror, the feeling that maybe I'd caused this? Or maybe I should talk about going to the pharmacy for the pregnancy test that confirmed my worst fear?

How about when drinking became my excuse to make awful choices? Like rationalizing that I was doing better than my friends. Or leaving my husband for a man who taught me to inject cocaine properly so I didn't kill myself.

Maybe I should start with those moments in the psych ward, begging for help with my depression and not realizing I wasn't even depressed—I was just consuming mass amounts of a depressant and couldn't stop.

No, let me step back a bit and start at the very beginning.

When I was a child, alcohol was the most tempting forbidden

fruit. Only adults could drink it—which made it feel like a sign of being grown-up—and the adults in my life seemed to think booze was a requirement for having fun. With anticipation, and also sometimes a bit of disgust, I watched them drink. Otherwise-normal adults would behave like crazy assholes at times and then be forgiven like nothing happened the next day because they said, "Sorry, I got drunk."

From the time I snuck those first bottles as a thirteen-year-old, I was hooked. Professional development days in junior high were spent at a friend's house drinking straight alcohol—usually vodka—until we all puked, passed out, or both, and then tried to get sober in time to go home. We would all meet at the friend's house first thing in the morning, not letting our parents know it was a day off school, or lying and saying we were working on homework together. One of us would get dressed up in order to look older and race to the liquor store to purchase the booze.

By high school, weekends were all about parties. If the parties were *really* wild, they'd go into Monday to help ease the hangovers. This continued through college, in large part because I never felt like I fit in anywhere. Alcohol let me "be myself" in social situations—or so I thought. With it, I could relax, feel accepted, and release inhibitions about being social.

At the time, my drinking seemed normal. It was "normal" to party until you puked or passed out. Everyone else was doing it, so I was no different. I didn't see a problem at all.

Of course, my drinking continued into adulthood. Some years it was really bad; other years it was "normal"—which means not totally out of control. I was able to hold down jobs and keep my friends. Gradually, though, I realized I didn't have a *stop* button when I was out drinking with friends or coworkers. Once the alcohol started flowing, I had no idea how to say "enough" before I passed out or ran out of booze.

As you can imagine, this led to a lot of embarrassing moments, but I'd learned that lesson from childhood well, and I was quick to say the magic words: "Sorry, I got drunk."

Mindboggling how those four little words make everything better.

In my late twenties, I discovered I was pregnant after being raped. I didn't know what to do, but I knew in my heart that I wanted this child, that this innocent being forming inside me was a chance to erase the bad and welcome the new.

I became a mother, alone.

My son is the best gift I've ever been given.

To this day, I've never told anyone how he was conceived. Even this story is written under a pseudonym. My son has grown up to be an incredibly kind, caring, and compassionate person. The circumstances of his birth don't reflect on him, and I don't ever want him to carry that burden. He's the light of my life.

Sadly, there's a lot I regret from his growing-up years. I considered myself a "high-functioning drinker" who could bounce right back after a night of extreme indulgence, who thought that it wouldn't affect my ability to parent, work, or succeed. I still thought it was "normal" to have so many drunken nights. My heart truly hurts when I look back at some of those choices.

In the most turbulent years, I got a DUI, lost custody of my son to my parents for a very short time, and found myself struggling to pay bills and keep food on the table—though there was always beer in the fridge. I got married and got a divorce. Through all this instability, my son has always loved me and stayed at my side.

Over time, drinking became my primary way to cope. It was my everything. I was getting drunk every single night and still didn't realize I had a problem. In the back of my mind, I knew it was an issue on some level, but I was still functioning, so I didn't think it was that bad. And, after all, I still had those four little words to fall back on whenever I behaved badly: "Sorry, I got drunk."

Then I found myself looking down at a gun in my hand, frantically searching for a bullet to end my life.

At that point, I couldn't deny that things weren't OK. That day was the beginning of my new life. It took me another year before I started searching in earnest for answers, but my brain was finally recognizing that there was a problem, and that I had to face it if I wanted to be here for my son.

I found *This Naked Mind* after someone suggested it on Facebook, and I figured it was worth a try. I ordered the book, but I wasn't really expecting it to change my life. It arrived, and I started reading with an open mind and a tentative hope for some answers.

It was revolutionary! I've now gone *years* without drinking, and a whole new life has begun for me.

I feel like a new person! I am a new person! I still struggle with social situations, and I'm still an introvert by nature. But now I know I have so much ahead of me. My regrets are starting to fade as I realize that holding onto them doesn't serve me, just like alcohol didn't serve me. I'm forgiving myself one step at a time.

My story isn't different from so many others, but I wrote it to say that there *is* another option. Setting down your "best friend" is scary, but it's the best gift you can give yourself. Loving yourself starts from within, and poisoning yourself with alcohol doesn't help you love yourself better. There is life beyond the drink, and it's beautiful!

I have so many dreams and plans I could detail here—things I'm working toward now that alcohol is out of my life. But, for me, the most important part of being alcohol-free is seeing how proud my son, the light of my life, is of me. That alone makes it worth it.

Much love to all, but most importantly, much love to you, Annie!

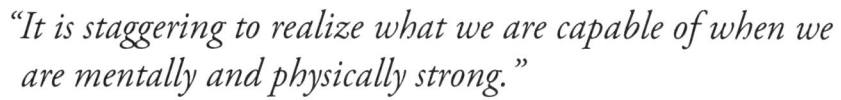

> "It is staggering to realize what we are capable of when we are mentally and physically strong."
>
> —Annie Grace, *This Naked Mind*

IT REALLY DOESN'T SUCK
Scott's Story

If I could tell my younger self one thing, it'd be this: "It really doesn't suck to quit drinking."

These days, I happily get up at 4:30 a.m. I spend those quiet morning hours reading, working out, and preparing for my day. My mind is clear when I get home after work. I'm achieving goals I used to only dream of. I'm constantly fine-tuning my life, pushing myself to greater heights of self-improvement. I'm better at networking, better at sales, better at being a husband and father.

Life is so much better than it used to be.

I was a "responsible" drinker. Yes, I drank every day, even though I knew it wasn't good for my health. Yes, all bets were off on the weekends. Yes, I knew my drinking habits weren't great. But I'd never gotten a DUI or come close to losing my family or torpedoing my job or any of the crazy horror stories I associated with problem drinking. Ever since I was a teenager, I'd known alcoholism ran in my family, but I always said, "That isn't me."

Until, one day, it seemed like it *was* me. And I didn't know what to do about it.

That realization kicked off four years of helplessness. Giving up drinking seemed scary as hell. What would I do with my time if I wasn't a drinker? How would I calm anxiety at professional events? How would I get through a neighborhood barbecue?

But I couldn't suppress the fear that my drinking was taking me in a bad direction. Others noticed, too. My wife brought it up to me more than once. So did other loved ones.

I wanted to stop. I didn't want to stop. I had my life together, right? So I didn't *need* to stop. But drinking wasn't making my life better. It was snowballing into turmoil and misery. Wash, rinse, repeat.

In the end, two things broke the stranglehold. I read *This Naked Mind*, and it stuck with me—something fundamentally changed inside me as a result of that book. I can't explain it, but I've never been able to see alcohol the same way. I also joined an online self-improvement group. While I was working to optimize my life with my new group—pushing to be the best version of myself—I was processing everything I'd read in *This Naked Mind*, turning it over and over in my head. Six months later, I realized I'd done all the easy stuff to improve my life. It was time to dig into the hard things.

Time to quit drinking. I picked up *This Naked Mind* again. Ready now.

I've got to get this out of my way if I'm going to keep growing, I told myself. It didn't matter if parties were going to be awkward or work events more difficult. I had to take that bold step and get that weight out of my life.

It wasn't the drag that I feared it would be. At work conferences, it became a superpower: everyone else would be drinking while I collected business cards and made appointments left and right. At cocktail parties, I'd just grab a soda water right away and sidestep all the awkward conversations—and no one noticed. My meetings now are more productive, and my conversations more substantial—at least on my side of the table.

After I got past the first few weeks, I even realized I didn't crave it anymore. Not picking up a beer was not a struggle for me. That's been the most freeing thing. It's freed my mental clarity, my energy levels, and so much of my time.

I laugh as I remember the question I once asked myself: *What would I do with my time if I wasn't a drinker?*

I now have more time to spend with my family, excel at my job, push myself to new heights, and help others in my online group along the journey to self-improvement—including helping others quit drinking. One of my hobbies has actually become studying the science around alcohol and addiction in general, especially different views of addiction. Now that I'm not drinking, I have time to read extensively in the field.

Another one of my favorite books on the subject is Marc Lewis's *The Biology of Desire*. In it, Lewis critiques the "disease theory" of addiction. Addiction, of course, bears a lot of resemblance to a disease at times, and calling it a disease is certainly better than calling it a moral failure or a weakness of character. But Lewis's book really resonated with me because it mapped so well onto my own experience.

At the risk of oversimplifying, synapses in our brains create pathways based on what we find rewarding. Those reward pathways create habits that can put us on the road to addiction when our reward centers are stimulated in unnaturally high ways—even if the brain is working exactly as it should be. But new pathways can always be forged and old ones abandoned.

So, when I explain this to my mentees, I like to compare the brain to a dense forest. If there's a path you take every day on the way home, that path is going to be pretty entrenched. But if you start taking a different path instead, you can blaze a new trail, and eventually that other one grows over. The brain's capacity to rewire itself is incredible.

Mentoring people on the road to freedom is far more validating and rewarding than having a drink ever was. And while I don't have a time machine to go back and tell my younger self, I can tell my mentees, who are newer to this path than I am: "It really doesn't suck to quit drinking."

"When you stop drinking, your brain will stop compensating and repair itself. You can again find pleasure in simply living—as you could before you ever started drinking."

—Annie Grace, *This Naked Mind*

SURGICALLY REMOVED
Jennifer's Story

This time is different. After a twenty-year cycle of binge drinking and trying to moderate, alcohol no longer controls me. And ever since I found my freedom from its grasp, I've felt a nagging to share my story. I'm a private person, so sharing this is scary. But I can't ignore this nudging because maybe my story can help someone else.

Alcohol has been in my life for two decades. The story usually looked like this: I tell myself I'll only have one or two drinks. Then I end up blacking out, unable to remember what I did the night before. I wake up the next morning, hungover and feeling guilty, but I pretend I feel fine because I don't want my husband and kids to know. I berate myself. Why am I so weak? So stupid? And above all, why can't I get this under control. Next come the promises: This was the last time. I'm not doing this again. Something has to change.

But it didn't change, not for a long time. Deep down, I didn't *want* to give up drinking. I wanted to grab drinks with coworkers or drink a beer at a Huskers game. I couldn't imagine admitting I had a problem, and I didn't want my friends to think I was no fun.

I tried moderating so many times with counseling, support

groups, willpower. But I craved it, and I always went back, falling harder and faster and deeper each time.

Eventually, I found an online group that offered a thirty-day challenge. I signed up for that—I wasn't going to make it permanent, of course, but I could give up drinking for thirty days.

I read posts from people in the group, and their stories were my story, their shame was my shame. For the first time, I didn't feel alone. I realized in the deepest part of myself that I wasn't the only one with a problem with alcohol—there were lots of others like me who questioned why they couldn't just "moderate."

To get through the thirty-day challenge, people in the group recommended drinking non-alcoholic beer and reading *This Naked Mind* by Annie Grace. And the book revolutionized my life. I discovered that my struggle wasn't because I was weak—that it's often the strongest, smartest, most successful people who drink more than they should. It made sense to me—in other areas of my life, I'm strong-willed to a fault. Why did I seem so weak-willed when it came to alcohol?

This Naked Mind gave me the answers I needed. I learned that my drinking was a battle between my conscious mind that wanted to cut back and my unconscious mind that hadn't changed its desires in the slightest. I was unconsciously rejecting my choice to drink less, and I didn't even know it. To change my relationship with alcohol, I first had to forgive myself. I had to accept that my inability to control my drinking was not a personality flaw, but that I'd started down the path of addiction from my very first drink in college, because alcohol is a highly addictive substance. Over the years, drinking had rewired my brain. While my conscious mind knew that my drinking was harmful, my unconscious belief that alcohol was bringing something positive to my life remained—guaranteeing that I'd crave drink after drink after drink. I felt like I was giving something up, that I was going to be missing out, that I was happier when I was drinking.

I don't understand how reading one book changed my life. But before I even finished, it was like my desire to drink had been surgically removed from my mind. I no longer crave alcohol. I no longer feel left out and angry when others are drinking. I actually *enjoy* going out with people even though I'm not drinking. I sip non-alcoholic beer and feel satisfied. I don't wake up with hangovers. I have mental clarity I haven't had in years. I am finally *free*!

Everyone's journey to addiction and their path out is different. And what worked for me won't help everyone. But if I can help one person change their relationship with alcohol and improve their life, then sharing my struggle was worth it.

"Once you shake the foundations of [your] conditioned beliefs, you can start to move forward without being hindered by unhelpful and unhealthy beliefs."

—Annie Grace, *The Alcohol Experiment*

DRAGGED DOWN
Lisa B.'s Story

I just completed a three-week health challenge. It ran on a points system, with points lost for cheating on the rules—which meant points lost if a participant drank any alcohol at all.

Two years ago, I wouldn't have even joined the challenge, even though I was health-focused. I ate mainly low-carb whole foods, ran every day, and was outwardly fit, but the idea of twenty-one days without my evening glass—or three—of wine would have seemed impossible.

I knew I was drinking more than was good for me. The alcohol was interfering with my sleep, and I was often awake at 3:00 a.m., vowing that the next day would be different. That I wouldn't drink at all. In the morning, fighting my foggy head and my disgust at my own behavior, I would haul myself out for a run, feeling like I was going to die. The wine was dragging down my running performance, but at least I was staying active. By 5:00 p.m., I'd be making deals with myself: I'd only have one glass. I'd only drink sitting down. I'd only drink mindfully.

So I'd have that first drink. And then, as they say, the drink would have a drink, and then the drink would have me.

I wasn't clear on how I'd ended up in this situation. All I'd really done was follow the script.

Hard day at work? Let's go for a drink—I deserve it.

Celebrating a milestone? Hey, break out the champagne!

Feeling tired and a bit down? A glass of wine will make me feel better.

As the years turned into decades, that glass of wine became a daily habit, a source of relief at the end of the day. And all too often, the glass turned into a bottle.

I never hit rock bottom. I never missed a day of work, crashed my car, or neglected my children, but my health started to suffer—despite my active lifestyle and attention to nutrition. By my mid-fifties, my blood pressure was getting too high. In my late fifties, my thyroid tests started to look dodgy, and I was diagnosed with low vitamin B12. I developed heartburn and tingling sensations in my fingers.

And, above all, my mental health and relationships were suffering. Alcohol had somehow become the most important relationship in my life—one I kept very private.

I couldn't see a way out. I'd tried so many times to use willpower to stop, and I'd never lasted even a day. But I was in no way prepared to label myself. I wasn't an addict or an alcoholic, so treatment programs weren't for me.

A turning point came a couple days after my father died. I was out for a night run and fell over the dog, injuring my leg. In the emergency room, I mentioned some chest pain. Once the doctor was satisfied that my heart was fine, she asked about my alcohol consumption.

For once, I was honest.

The information from that ER visit got sent to my regular doctor. She has a particular interest in addiction, and she followed up with me—not believing me when I said, "Don't worry, I've got this."

Since I adamantly refused a referral to addiction services—after all, that was not me—there wasn't much she could do for me. But it forced me to admit I had a problem, and one that only I could fix.

You know how the internet seems to read your thoughts? I don't think I ever even googled anything about alcohol, but Facebook started to feed me ads about a program called This Naked Mind. At first, I ignored it. I had no faith it would work. Why spend money on something like that when I really just needed to will myself to drink less?

But then the ads started talking about something called The Alcohol Experiment, starting January 1. Really, what did I have to lose?

It took me a couple days to get my head around it. Because of the time difference, January 1 in the States is January 2 in New Zealand, where I live. That was a good excuse to put it off a day. On January 2, I was busy and still grasping for excuses, but I only had one glass of wine. A minor stressor reared its head on January 3, and I drank a whole bottle to deal with it.

Then came the hangover on the morning of January 4. I rolled over in bed, absolutely miserable and exhausted. And I wasn't just physically tired—I was tired all the way to my soul, tired of the wine, tired of the hangovers, tired of being dragged down.

It was time to commit to quitting.

I started reading the book, caught up on the videos provided with the program, and joined the associated Facebook group that connected me with two thousand people around the world doing this Experiment with me. As I worked through the material, I made two lists, as Annie Grace suggested. I found I had a very, very long list of reasons why I wanted to quit drinking and a very short list of reasons why I drank. Perhaps most importantly, I sat down with my husband, talked honestly about my alcohol consumption, and asked for his support for the next thirty days.

That was the beginning of my sober life.

That month was a revelation. I discovered I wasn't alone. I learned that my brain was working exactly as it was intended to—that our brains are hard-wired for survival in a very different environment than what we live in today. I accepted that my problem drinking wasn't my fault, but it was my responsibility. I developed skills to manage my habitual thoughts and tactics to survive the cravings. And I connected with a community of intelligent, successful, thoughtful people, who shared their experiences and supported each other through the hard times.

At the end of the month, I made the choice to continue to live alcohol-free. It was a joyful decision, with no feelings of hardship or deprivation. I'd lost nothing and gained the world.

Systems help keep me on track, and I knew that I needed one as I cemented this new way of living. So I followed up the January challenge with a three-month This Naked Mind intensive program, then signed up for 100 Days of Lasting Change. In total, that gave me seven months of support through daily videos and online communities.

By the time I finished those, my brain was really, truly rewired. Now, further down the road, my life is so much better that it's hard for me to describe it!

I'm free from the physical results of drinking, but I'm also free from self-loathing and fear. I have more money to spend on holidays and on treats that really give me joy, and more time to spend doing things I love. I'm working on healing and growing my relationships with my family, and I'm even on a new career path in my sixties!

Because I no longer drink to numb my feelings and deal with conflict and stress, I've had to develop healthy coping skills, and I practice deliberate, daily self-care. In fact, I've discovered that much of the conflict and stress in my life was caused by alcohol!

Why would I ever want to drink alcohol again? It's just an addictive poison. There are so many other wonderful things to eat and drink and do! Things that boost our health and give us true life and joy.

I'm running after those things, and I'm so glad wine isn't dragging me down.

"Real human connection comes from being vulnerable."

—Annie Grace, *The Alcohol Experiment*

THE PEOPLE THAT WE ARE
Lorraine's Story

My father was an alcoholic. He left me, my mom, and my sister when I was young. He's been sober now for thirty years, and I do have a relationship with him, but back then it was tough—all because of alcohol.

In high school, I ended up moving in with my binge-drinking grandparents. They were from Oklahoma and Arkansas, and if I smelled alcohol on my grandfather's breath on a Saturday, I knew they were going to start throwing things by the time the weekend was over. They'd have huge fights that I—at age fourteen or fifteen—would have to try to break up.

I determined that I was never going to drink alcohol.

But I worked in the fast-food industry, and my boss wanted to be "the cool boss." So he invited the employees—many of us were sixteen, seventeen, or eighteen—over to party, and the alcohol was free flowing. He didn't mean it to be insidious, but it was the beginning of my foray into the party lifestyle. When I got a little older, I realized I was gay and started getting into drugs—although not really into alcohol. But I got a DUI in the late '80s, and there weren't many options for treatment programs—so I had to go to AA. I remember showing up, looking around, and thinking, *I don't even drink*. Hearing everyone's stories, I concluded that alcohol could really mess you up. But once I got off the drugs, I still started my slow slide into alcohol.

I began drinking in my twenties and thirties but really ramped it up in my forties. My now-sober father told me that alcohol was a poison, but I didn't want to hear it. I don't even remember my fiftieth birthday. Alcohol stole that whole day from me. It's stolen a lot of days and a lot of joy. I love to be active—riding my bike, especially—but it was so hard to convince myself to go outside when I was hungover, which was often.

I realized it was becoming serious, because I was sneaking alcohol. I'd take a shot out of the freezer or hide a bottle in the office or the bathroom or in my nightstand. I always had a ready excuse to justify myself when I felt guilty—I'm bigger than my wife, so I need a little more to get the same high. Finally, I told my wife that I thought I might have problems with alcohol. But we pushed it aside and decided it wasn't *too* bad. After all, I wasn't at rock bottom. I was still functioning at a high level. It got brushed aside because I wasn't able to be fully honest with her about how much I was drinking. She knew I was having a little more than I should, but she had no idea how bad it really was.

Alcohol began taking up more and more of my headspace. I'd schedule social activities around where we could drink the most, and I was always thinking ahead to my next drink. I couldn't go a week without it, unless I was deathly ill. Eventually, I talked to my doctor about a naltrexone prescription, which keeps you from getting a high from alcohol. She gave me the prescription, along with a book on moderation.

Neither helped. I discontinued the naltrexone quickly because I didn't *like* that I didn't feel a buzz when I drank. And the book just seemed too complicated. I'm an accountant, and even I had a hard time following all the numbers I was supposed to track—number of drinks, number of hours, blood-alcohol percentage.

So I set the prescription and the book aside and kept drinking. My lab work was getting dicey—especially my glucose and triglycerides. Eventually, I stopped getting tested for over a year because the numbers were steadily worsening. And I knew it was because of alcohol. I just didn't know how to stop.

Last December, my wife and I went to a movie theater with some friends. Nowadays, movie theaters have full bars. So we showed up early to drink before the movie, and I was about four drinks in when our friends arrived. I expected our friends to order cocktails—they were the biggest drinkers in our social group besides me. But they declined. When I asked them about it, they said they hadn't had a drink in months.

"Really?" I asked, astonished. "That's incredible."

After the movie, I asked one of the friends how they'd quit.

She responded, "Just read Annie Grace's book. I can't explain it. I'm not even going to go into it. Just read *This Naked Mind*."

My wife and I went out for another beer afterward, and I woke up the next morning with a horrible hangover. I felt awful. But I remembered the name "Annie Grace," so I got on my Kindle and downloaded the book. I read it in two or three days. And I haven't had a drink since that beer after the movie.

Quitting felt like magic—because I believe in science. That was the key that helped me buy into the approach: it's scientific. If your subconscious believes one thing, your conscious mind can't convince it to change just by saying something once. You have to go through a relearning process in which your brain is rewired.

I've had a few twinges of cravings here and there, especially at friends' houses where alcohol was being served, but by and large it's been unbelievably easy. I expected I wouldn't have fun, that I wouldn't be funny anymore, that I'd be boring. But everything is so much better. I like myself so much more.

When I went to get my blood work done three months after I stopped drinking, my glucose had gone down twenty points, and my triglycerides had gone down fifty points. Right there is a testament to how much damage we do to our bodies by drinking. Not to mention the money I've saved! When I added it all up—$12 for a six-pack, $10 per drink at a restaurant—I realized I'd saved $2000. I should take that money and go on a vacation!

Brain change is an ongoing process, and we're bombarded by so many messages about alcohol every day. One of the most interesting parts of *This Naked Mind* talks about advertising. The chapter told me to not stop drinking yet but to pay attention to all the commercials, all the ads, all the times I saw people drink on TV, and all the times I heard people talk about alcohol positively. Once you start paying attention, you can't unhear it. The messages are everywhere. It was a huge eye-opener for me. So now, I consciously try to counteract those messages. I listen to the *This Naked Mind* podcast. I've reread the book a couple of times. And I listen to people's stories. Because I think that human connection—hearing other people's stories and telling our own—is the way we grow and survive and become better people.

If I could say one thing to a person struggling with drinking, it would be this: It's just false thinking to believe you can't have fun without alcohol or that you're going to be a different person. Without alcohol, you become the person you *really* are. And that's what we should all strive to be. Not trying to change ourselves into the person we think we should be.

We need to be who we truly are. And you can't be that if you're drunk all the time.

"There is no inexplicable defect in our personalities, no elusive flaw in our bodies. Alcohol is simply a highly addictive drug."

—Annie Grace, *This Naked Mind*

NOBODY KNEW BUT ME
Grace's Story

I've had a lovely life. No drama or difficult childhood or troubled parents. I've been very blessed. A thirty-four-year marriage to a great guy who loves me. My sons, their partners, and two granddaughters are the lights of my life. Wonderful jobs. Creative pursuits—painting, mostly—that excite me.

That's why I'm writing this story. You see, my alcohol addiction has been so puzzling to me, and I think that's because people assume all "problem drinkers" are the same. I recently read a claim that alcohol addiction is about dealing with deep pain. I think that's BS. Certainly, there are plenty of heavy drinkers who are dealing with tragic pasts, but some of us just fell into the trap without a "reason" we can point to. It's really kind of boring in many ways—no trauma or hardship or wild and dangerous drinking stories.

In hindsight, I think I used alcohol (and nicotine) as a way to be rebellious and wild while also trying to be perfect and "good." To the outside world, I've always been a happy, strong, confident person. Alcohol slowly chipped away at that self-image and made me feel like I was living a lie.

Despite outward appearances, my drinking felt like it was out of my control. It made me feel bad. It made me anxious and scared of dying or being incapacitated. It made me ashamed and worried that I was missing out. It made me feel stuck and stupid and weak. It made me stop trying new things. It made my mornings fuzzy and sad. It made me dislike and mistrust myself. It made me lose hope. It made me cry. It took pleasure from things that should have been pleasurable. It hijacked my life. And nobody knew it but me.

I'm fifty-eight. I've been drinking since I was sixteen—sometimes a little, sometimes a lot. From the beginning, I smoked cigarettes when I drank. The only time I stopped completely was when I was pregnant. Others didn't know how much I was drinking—it's easy to hide when you can down half a bottle of vodka with almost no outward effects. I was able to keep myself under control when I was out with friends. Drinking at home became my "thing."

A few years ago, my fifty-year-old brother died. The cause of death: alcohol. After years of heavy, heavy drinking, he died alone, in pain, estranged from everyone he knew, including his four children. It broke my heart, but it didn't stop me. If anything, I probably drank more in the years following.

I was an every-night drinker. I didn't drink until I blacked out, but I did have what I called "brown outs," where things just got kind of fuzzy for me. I could remember that I watched a particular show but not exactly what had happened on it. (Who got voted off the island? Hell if I know.)

I tried to quit a couple times a year—it usually lasted a week or two before I ended up in bed, drunk-writing in my journal about how much I wanted to stop. I lay awake for hours, pleading with God to show me how. I knew—just *knew*—that there had to be a way that would be joyful and easy and not a depressing carousel ride of meetings and deprivation and misery.

Then I found *This Naked Mind*.

This book was, without any doubt, the direct answer to my prayers. I finally stopped drinking and have been grateful every single day since. I'm done. I've escaped. I'm free. And it was, for the most part, a joyful experience.

I know that some people don't like the word "never," but I am *thrilled* to say "never." I no longer want or need to drink, and I don't have to spend any mental energy on that decision.

My husband is still a drinker. He drinks every night and has no intention of stopping. When I first quit, that was really hard for me—the biggest point of pain in the otherwise serene experience of finding freedom. To see him pour his nightly cocktail and then go outside for a cigarette? Sometimes I could hardly stand to be in the same room as him, and I found myself avoiding him. I'm sure he (legitimately) thought I'd go back to it as I had so many times before. He's never questioned his drinking. It's a given part of his life, and he's never worried that he's dependent or drinking too much.

I was frustrated and indignant about this when I first quit. How *dare* he keep going while I was doing this important and difficult thing? I bring this up because I hear this so much in the online community, this anger with partners who still drink. And here's what happened to me: after almost four months, it stopped bothering me. Not drinking is my choice, not his. Would I like him to quit? Of course. But I've come to the realization that he's a kind man who loves me very much and is good to me and others. A huge, unexpected bonus of quitting is that I find myself feeling much kinder toward him than I used to. I think it's because I like myself better without all the guilt and shame and anxiety. Sobriety has allowed me to relax and become more accepting.

When I was drinking and smoking, I would sometimes imagine a vivid picture of what my life could be like. Now, I'm putting one sober foot in front of the other, and that vision is starting to come true. I don't know all the details yet, but life feels exciting and hopeful again. I actually feel, at fifty-eight, that I have a new life. It seems like a miracle.

With all my heart, I wish this feeling for everyone who struggles. I've re-written this at least six times because I want so much to get it right. Not because I care what anyone thinks of me—I'm anonymous, anyway—but because I hope that even one person recognizes themselves and feels hope that their life can be so much better without alcohol.

Because I know it can.

"If we truly want to combat loneliness, we need to be courageous enough to be raw and real. We need to talk about our struggles. The more I show up with my real stories, the more people come back with their own real stories. We're all struggling together. The more we pretend we have it all together, the more we push other people away."

—Annie Grace, *The Alcohol Experiment*

HUNTED BY FEAR
Carolyn's Story

BTK.

Ask anyone who grew up in Wichita in the '70s. They can tell you what those three threatening letters stand for. I was just a child on January 15, 1974, when the BTK serial killer murdered his first victims, four members of the Otero family—Joseph and Julie Otero, and two of their children. The Oteros' teenage son came home later that day and discovered the bodies.

So began my story of fear. Two blocks were all that separated my family from the Oteros' house. Two blocks away, evil had stalked the innocent. Why them? Why not us? Who would be next? The world wasn't safe anymore. I lost a bit of my own innocence that day and found long-term anxiety in its place.

The man went on to kill a total of ten people from 1974 to 1991 and wasn't arrested until 2005. His brazen correspondence with authorities and local newspapers was almost as sinister as the killings themselves—he sent taunting letters describing the details of his crimes.

Simple childhood games like hide-and-seek became sources of torment. I wanted to play outside with the older kids, but inevitably one of them would yell, "BTK is coming to get you!" I gave myself away every time by sprinting from my hiding place to my front door.

In 1996, I gave birth to my first child. The anxiety sank its claws deeper into my soul. After all, the world wasn't safe. What if someone hurt my children? I spent my waking moments ensuring they were safe and out of trouble. Nights were worse, an ongoing nightmare of fear. I'd jolt awake and sneak into my sons' bedrooms again and again to make sure they were still there.

I'm a Christian. I believe in the power of prayer. But I didn't think God "got" it. He couldn't save me from the energy of my mind, or so I thought at the time. Only one thing could help: wine.

Inside a bottle, I found my new best friend. She quieted the racing thoughts. She provided safety, comfort, and a place to land. I could drink away the compulsive need to protect and the gnawing feeling that the world was uncertain and insecure.

But her love came at a great cost. Like any narcissist who only serves herself, she came into my life promising comfort, but she stole more and more and more. She took precious time from my husband and boys. Most of all, she stole my health. Over time, hypothyroidism and adrenal burnout became new words in my vocabulary. Depression, migraines, and weight gain accompanied these diagnoses.

I tried everything to improve my health—everything other than giving up my precious wine. But one morning, about two decades into my drinking life, everything changed. I was struggling with depression and not feeling well, and a friend said, "It's all in your mindset."

Those words struck me just the right way. They were life changing. I decided enough was enough. From there on out, I resolved, I'd change my mindset and stop drinking.

I white-knuckled my way through those first three months of my new alcohol-free lifestyle. It didn't feel like freedom. I wasn't truly living; I was merely surviving. It wasn't sustainable. Cue struggle, determination, and prayer. So much prayer. Did God "get" it? Did anyone "get" it?

Then, through an online source, I found Annie Grace and immediately ordered *This Naked Mind*. I read it twice in two weeks. I knew I'd found my answer. Her methods blew my mind. God had sent me someone who "got" it.

Annie's method allows us to learn, grow, and change our relationship with alcohol at our own pace. She provides the facts. With the right blend of psychology and neuroscience research, her no-scare tactics and no-nonsense truths are turning the recovery community on its head.

This Naked Mind taught me that I wasn't flawed or broken, at least not more than any other human. I wasn't a detestable person because I'd spent so many years trying to drink my fear away. A cunning substance had deceived me.

My life has immeasurably changed in the years since I read *This Naked Mind*. My health has gotten better day by day and is still improving. My relationships with friends and family are stronger than ever. I'm doing things I never dreamed of, and above all, I find myself able to manage the anxiety that's haunted me since childhood. I often have to pinch myself after getting eight hours of sleep, because I hadn't gotten a full night of uninterrupted sleep since BTK murdered my neighbors.

The future looks bright these days, instead of frightening. I'm not afraid of the shadows. The world may be uncertain, but I'm optimistic and hopeful.

Bring it on.

"Life has so much variety to offer, and we need all our senses intact in order to experience it."

—Annie Grace, *The Alcohol Experiment*

I JUST DIDN'T WANT TO DRINK POISON ANYMORE
Marc's Story

My first experience with alcohol was probably like most people's. When I was fifteen and in high school, I was offered some high-quality malt liquor. I remember vomiting as the room spun around me, and I said I'd never drink again. Of course, that didn't last. I drank occasionally throughout much of high school, but it was mostly experimentation at that point. My heavy drinking didn't start until I was twenty-one and a junior in college.

By then, I had friends who were into the party lifestyle. We'd head down to Sixth Street every Thursday through Sunday—getting pretty much wasted every night. Based on some of the scares I had that first year of heavy drinking, I probably shouldn't be alive today.

While celebrating St. Patrick's Day and March Madness, I got behind the wheel after way too many drinks. I thought I was putting the car in drive to exit a Toys R Us parking lot, but I actually put it in reverse and slammed into a light pole. The impact caused me to switch the car to drive and jump the ditch that separated the parking lot from a four-lane road. My front bumper fell off as I pulled into a parking lot on the other side of the street.

Miraculously, no one was hurt. I was just dazed, with no idea what had happened. We weren't quite sure how we'd even gotten there until our friends in the other car pulled up alongside us. They explained the airborne, Dukes of Hazzard-style jump across the ditch. My friend drove my car home with the bumper in the trunk.

That's a moment I'm not proud of. If I'd been cited for a DUI, my life might have taken a much different path, but I didn't get caught. I just had to face the shame of telling my mother and my girlfriend—who is now my wife of fifteen years.

Even after that, I didn't swear off alcohol. Instead, I rationalized how I got to that point. I hadn't eaten enough that day. Hadn't drunk enough water while pounding the shots. Probably shouldn't have had that last shot that put me over the top. I did vow to never drink and drive again, but I can't say I held one hundred percent to that, as buzzed driving is drunk driving.

After graduating, I got a great job in high-tech software sales. It required a lot of entertaining and nights out—I vividly remember someone telling me, "You have to drink to be in this profession." Company events centered around booze, from afternoon kegs to happy hours to club trips. Alcohol was simply a part of the job. As long as you showed up, did your job, and didn't appear drunk during work hours, nobody thought much of it.

During this time, I never had another incident like the one in college, but my drinking continued to escalate. On sales kickoffs in Vegas, we went to the local drugstore to load up on Pedialyte so we could drink more. By the second trip, the store had gotten clever and moved the Pedialyte next to the alcohol. I proudly took a picture, feeling like we'd helped start that trend of pre-gaming with electrolytes.

Due to this job, I started hanging out with guys who drank a lot more than I did. That, of course, led me to drink more—while claiming I had it under control because I didn't drink as much as my friends and coworkers. Of course, this was my subconscious rationalizing my habits, and it didn't reflect reality.

These guys and I would take trips where we'd easily knock back a couple cases of beer. I'd puke my guts out and sometimes end up in the ER with dehydration. On one trip, we were out on a boat, and I was tossed overboard when my buddy made a sharp turn. When I got back onto the boat, I realized I'd hurt my neck, so I downed a few painkillers alongside the eighteen or so beers. I spent the next day sleeping fitfully on the bathroom floor, worried I was going to die.

At some point, I decided I needed to cut back on the alcohol, but I wasn't able to moderate. I'd wake up every morning between three and four, depressed because I slipped up and drank the night before. I'd think of the history of addiction in my family—of how my brother lost his life to drugs. Then I'd swear to not do it again that day. It never stuck.

As the afternoon wore on, I'd start to get that tickle in the back of my mind that booze was just around the corner. Concerns about addiction wore off. Sure, I had a family history, but I didn't have "that personality." I was in complete control. And so I'd drink again.

I did once manage a Dry January—almost. I made it three weeks, anyway. But we had a long weekend in Belize coming up for my birthday, so I decided I needed to prime my liver for that. I couldn't go there without the tolerance I'd built up, so I rationalized drinking the week before we left. The whole ordeal actually made my drinking worse. I'd starved my body of alcohol and then doubled down when the three weeks were over.

Of course, growing work stress didn't help. I started turning to booze even more. I would literally daydream about that first sip of alcohol that I'd get to have when the day was over. And when it finally came, I felt like I deserved it for putting up with what was going on at work. One vodka soda or old-fashioned would quickly turn into three or four. Weekends became excuses for drinking instead of time enjoyed with my wife and kids. My runs to the liquor store grew more frequent, but I kept ignoring it. I didn't want to admit to myself that I was no longer in control.

I can't pinpoint exactly what made me finally say enough is enough, but I think my upcoming birthday played a big role. I'm turning forty soon, and my health wouldn't last if I continued to drink. I bought a stationary bike and got hooked on it. I loved the rush of energy! And hangovers made it hard to ride and give it my all. With how much I was working to get healthier, the thought of pouring more alcohol down my throat started to lose its appeal, especially after reading *This Naked Mind*.

I read the book in about a day, even though it advises you to space it out. What can I say? I'm a rule-breaker and couldn't put it down. As I learned that I could get out of the alcohol trap without a twelve-step program, I was inspired. And when I looked at my bike and thought about my health journey, I just didn't want to drink poison anymore. The evidence of alcohol's harmful health impacts is strong, and I don't want that to be my future.

My days since quitting have been so much more fun. I enjoy my kids more, I wake up feeling refreshed and with a better outlook on life, and I can have fun with friends without a booze-infested, hangover-triggering weekend. I'm happier and healthier and more energetic.

Most of all, I'm looking forward to the future and all the years to come.

"While it's not easy to be different, it is good. And you are strong."

—Annie Grace, *This Naked Mind*

11,000 CALORIES AND £240
Ria's Story

I didn't even notice I'd started drinking excessively. It's like that metaphor of the pitcher plant that Annie Grace talks about in her book. I started slowly, picking up the pace more and more without realizing it. Before I knew it, I was so far in that I couldn't see a way out.

I was trapped.

When I was twelve or thirteen, I was allowed to drink beer at home. I'd sip one can throughout the evening. I didn't like the taste. I hated it, even. But I remember feeling like I should force it down, to be cool. To be like my older brothers, their friends, my parents. All drinkers, all advertising it to me as a young teenager. It seemed like it was something fun and exciting. Something everyone did. Something I'd better do, too, if I wanted to be normal.

My stepfather died from liver disease, brought on by alcohol, when I was sixteen. It happened only a few years after his father had died of the same thing. We lost him on Christmas Eve, in the living room, on a hospital bed in front of the Christmas tree. We raised a glass to him on Christmas Day.

The irony.

After that, I started drinking more, going out clubbing with friends. I don't remember hangovers back then. I had an endless stamina for a boozy night out, and I dabbled in drugs too. Speed, ecstasy, cocaine—chasing the buzz that I craved. Looking back, I don't know how I made it through school with good grades.

The drugs stopped when I went away to university. I'd started having panic attacks and was scared all the time, particularly about dying, so the thought of an accidental overdose filled me with dread. The drinking, however, persisted. It seemed normal to drink every day, to drink until I puked. I was slipping further and further into the pitcher plant.

The first time I wondered if I was drinking too much, I was twenty years old and returning from a holiday to Greece. I got home, and the alcohol cravings were intense. I drove to the shop and bought beers to drink at home alone. It was a warning sign. But I didn't try to get out of the trap.

Ever since, my life has been a series of alcohol-related ups and downs. Feeling unhappy, drinking heavily, tired all the time. Sometimes life was a little better—I was still tired but only on the weekends. But the bottom line was that I was a drinker—a big drinker, a fast drinker, a lone drinker, someone who drinks to relax, to have fun. I've injured myself drunk, vomited on new carpets, upset loved ones, embarrassed myself at work parties ... I was addicted.

And I knew it.

The bizarre thing is that I'm so concerned about my health. I exercise, read, eat healthy food, and try to look after myself—so why did I never consider giving up booze? It was always there—the idea of it—lurking in my mind. But deep down, I think I knew that getting off the roller coaster that alcohol had brought to my life meant giving it up completely, forever. And, until recently, that thought was scary. I'd be missing out. I'd never have fun again.

Turns out, I was wrong to worry. When it finally became clear that I needed to take that step, I read *This Naked Mind*. I no longer drink. I feel stronger mentally and physically. I'm happier and more at ease. I'm sleeping better than I have in years. Seeing more clearly. Relaxing more. Enjoying people's company more. I think they're enjoying my company more too!

My health is improving, my skin is clearer, my eyes are brighter. My workouts are more rewarding, and I'm seeing new results—which shouldn't surprise me, because I estimated I've saved myself eleven thousand calories and £240 every single *month* by not drinking.

Most of all, that nagging hatred for myself has disappeared.

One thing that really stuck in my head when I was reading *This Naked Mind* was the idea of being a child, before alcohol, and feeling happy. Enjoying life . . . and everything being OK. That image is what has driven me to this point. I don't want to drink again. I want to be free, like I was as a child. This Experiment has opened my eyes to the possibilities and is driving me forward every day to new experiences. Not through willpower but through choice.

I'm realizing it's possible to make this decision and still enjoy life. We've been conditioned to think that's not true, but it is. I'm proof of that, as are all those like me, who are choosing not to drink because we believe we are better off without it. I'm making a promise to myself to carry on, take every day as it comes, and keep driving forward. Thank you to *This Naked Mind* for helping me get to this point—a place I never thought I'd reach!

"You see your entire life, long and healthy, stretch out before you. You are proud. You have done something amazing. You are excited to enjoy this remarkable life and all of the many, wonderful human experiences it holds."

—Annie Grace, *This Naked Mind*

ONE HUNDRED PERCENT ME
Laura's Story

I spontaneously sobered up two years ago, seemingly overnight, at the same time I came out of the closet. At first, I was perplexed as to why I didn't crave alcohol. How could I be truly at peace with the idea of never drinking again? But now I think I understand.

It started with a courageous conversation. My bubble of lies burst, and I began anew. Until recently, I was quite unsure whether I'd truly stopped *alcohol*, or whether I'd just stopped straight sex—the reason I recklessly used alcohol. Regardless of the answer, life is so much better now—I'm fully myself, living with a mind and body free from self-destruction and not looking back. But reading *This Naked Mind* brought so much clarity to a mystifying aspect of my new life, a life free from deep self-loathing masked by fake happiness.

When I came out as a lesbian, I freed myself from fifteen-plus years of pain, of sexual self-abuse, of brutal shame. Now, even though I go to moms' nights out at wine bars and date regular drinkers, I have zero desire to partake in any alcohol consumption. That stumped me every time I stopped to ponder it. Would this sudden success hold up forever? Was I a ticking time bomb? If quitting was so hard for most people, why was it a breeze for me?

Maybe I hadn't really been addicted to my regular binge sessions. Maybe I drank to numb myself and repress my sexuality. Now, I think coming out freed me from the reasons I needed to escape: a painful cycle of self-harm with sex that wasn't right for me.

In chapter ten of *This Naked Mind*, I learned that my inhibitions against sleeping with men—my one partner, once a boyfriend and then a husband of thirteen years—were in place to protect me from harming myself. I inadvertently defied my inhibitions by drinking to "fit in" with my straight boyfriend (though I did question my sexuality in college). He liked it when I drank with him, so that "liquid confidence" made the physical connection easier. Really, I was dying inside to break free and find out who I really was meant to be. I felt trapped in a half-truth, and my only comfort was beer.

Drinking was an easy way to not care much about sex or how "right" it felt to be sexual with a partner whose company I greatly enjoyed during the less-intimate moments, when we were good friends and had fun hanging out. Drinking infused all of our social interactions, and alcohol was always there to numb me when we had sex. By the time we started a family several years in, I was so used to just giving in and so estranged from any sense of true self that I didn't even need to be drunk to partake in sex. I just had to slip into that numb, detached state of being and let it happen, then drink afterward to deal with it.

Inhibitions serve an important purpose. They help us avoid risks, such as marrying and starting a family under false pretenses. But I washed away my inhibitions with beer to avoid the pain of truth-telling, ultimately repressing my sexuality and any semblance of self-respect in favor of numbness.

Once I decided I was no longer afraid to be my real self, one hundred percent me, I no longer desired anything "poisonous" that would alter me. Reading *This Naked Mind* helped me see that my need to be my true self is only possible without alcohol. Until I read the book, I thought maybe someday I'd want to drink in moderation, but I now see that I have a gift in this lack of desire to drink. It feels like a miracle. I'm learning to love myself for who I am, and I clearly see that alcohol has no place in my story as I move forward into who I was always meant to be.

"As long as you're alive, you'll never run out of chances to regain control of your life. The only way to fail at this is to give up and stop trying."

—Annie Grace, *The Alcohol Experiment*

A SAFE PRESENCE
Brandy's Story

Pregnant? I felt lightheaded as my white-knuckled fingers gripped the test. I couldn't be pregnant. I was only nineteen. And more than morning sickness fueled the nausea that rocked my body. Though I couldn't put my finger on *why*, I knew something was off in my relationship. And now there was a baby, which in my mind meant I had to stay with my boyfriend.

I'd grown up incredibly sheltered. My parents weren't particularly religious, but they were old-fashioned, and my mom had kept me in a bubble. When I turned eighteen and escaped that bubble, I didn't have the tools or street smarts to make good decisions.

It started spring break of senior year—I went on a trip to Myrtle Beach with a couple friends and the liquor that my sister-in-law bought us. Within a year, I'd escalated from alcohol and cigarettes to marijuana, unprotected sex, and even harder drugs.

And then there I was—nineteen and pregnant.

In some counterintuitive way, my teenage pregnancy saved me, I think. It meant I had to get off substances for nine months, and it diverted me permanently from hard drugs. But, looking back, I was in an abusive relationship and too naïve to see what was going on. It didn't seem like leaving was an option, because I had a child with him.

I started smoking and drinking again as soon as my daughter was born, and my partner and I drifted through life, numbing ourselves, drinking through the day, and partying at night. The first turning point came when I went to counseling. I was telling the therapist about my partner's crazy, manipulative behavior and then said, "We're planning our wedding."

My counselor's eyes widened. "Are you sure you want to do that?"

"I . . . don't have to?"

It was the first time someone had told me that I didn't have to marry him. I was twenty-two.

We'd broken up before, but this time was different. I was calm. I knew it was really over. It was a calculated decision I'd made with a cool head, not an impassioned screaming match in the parking lot.

To celebrate, I started partying whenever I didn't have my daughter. Four months later, I got a DWI. That was my second turning point, because I lost my job. I had a child. It felt dire. I knew I had to get responsible—at the very least, I had to not drink and drive.

So I found Jesus. Fundamentalist Christianity became my salvation. Though I was a little put off by what felt like patriarchy, I didn't care enough. I couldn't do life on my own. If it was left up to me, I'd destroy myself.

Once I made up my mind, I stopped binge drinking, stopped having sex with random people I met in bars, stopped smoking pot. By the following summer, I'd even quit smoking cigarettes. I was working as a housekeeper for the church. I'd done a turnaround, and things were going well.

Then I got the worst news of my life.

My mom was watching my daughter while I'd gone to help an elderly couple rake leaves. When I got back, she pulled me inside.

My daughter had confided that she'd been hurt by a family member on her dad's side.

Panic flooded me. I couldn't breathe. My daughter had been hurt. How could I keep her safe? I was still so young. How could I fix this? How could I clean up a mess that wasn't mine? I was the screwed-up one. How could I be what my daughter needed me to be in this situation?

But I also knew I didn't have a choice. I had to. She had no one else. If this had come out a year earlier, I don't know what would have happened. Because I don't know if I would have had the strength within myself to do what I needed to do for her.

The church rallied around us, and they were so supportive during that dark time. And I pulled myself together. A little while later, I got married. We had a dry wedding—my husband has never liked the taste of alcohol, so he doesn't drink at all. So I thought that part of my life was over, that I'd left that person I used to be behind. But a corner of my heart was always afraid I'd go back. That left to my own devices, I'd screw up again.

Over time, our faith evolved, and we moved into a more progressive Christianity, not focused on dogma, and I became interested in alternative spirituality. But as we left behind our black-and-white thinking, new possibilities opened on the horizon. I found myself struggling. *Was* it OK to drink? If there's so much gray in all these other areas, surely drinking wasn't a matter of right versus wrong. After all, I reasoned, my big problem had been pot. Surely it would be fine to drink as long as I stayed away from pot.

And it *was* fine, for a while. Or it felt fine. Because I didn't realize how quickly it was escalating. It wasn't long before I couldn't remember the last time I hadn't had a glass of wine in the evening.

A year or two later, I went out with a coworker one night, and we had a couple of drinks. When we got back to the car, he tried to climb on top of me. I was devastated, convinced I'd done something wrong. Even though I was a feminist, even though I'd majored in sociology, I wasn't able to name what had happened "assault."

My husband had to recognize it for me. When I steeled up my courage and confessed what "I'd done," he didn't treat me as though I'd cheated. He asked me good questions and helped me realize that it had been an unwanted advance that I had not invited, that I'd stopped once I'd realized what was going on. That it was an assault.

We started going back to counseling, and my counselor had an addiction background. She never pressed me to quit drinking, but she recognized that I wasn't in a good place with alcohol. "Are you sure this feels good and safe and comfortable?" she asked me once.

I nodded. "It's fine. It was his fault."

I wasn't ready to quit. But I did decide to take my husband when I went out drinking, so he could make sure I didn't do anything stupid.

But last year, my husband went to Seattle for school for five months, and I was finishing up my master's degree while working, doing an internship, and being a mom. I was tired. My best friend and I went out salsa dancing to blow off some steam. And we drank a *lot*.

I don't remember what happened next, but my friend tells me that we were trying to head home, and a couple guys came up to us and said, "Hey, want to go around the corner to see a friend?"

Our drunk selves said, "Yeah! That sounds great."

"Around the corner" ended up being his car, and he'd taken us twenty minutes from the bar when he got pulled over for drinking and driving. As he got his DWI, my friend whispered, "I don't think we should be here. We need to go."

That's when I started to come to, and I have patchy memories of the rest of the night. We got out of the car and took an Uber home. I puked on the front steps and somehow made it up to my bedroom.

When I woke up the next day, I was mortified. What might

have happened if he hadn't gotten pulled over? I could have died. I could have been raped. Thank God none of that happened. Thank God for that officer.

As I thought back over that night, over the night my coworker assaulted me, over all the stupid decisions I'd made while drinking, I decided I was done. And I want to say this part as delicately and precisely as I can, because it was absolutely not my fault that I was assaulted by my coworker. It would not have been my fault if I'd been raped or killed that awful night I went salsa dancing. The responsibility for such crimes begins and ends with the perpetrators. But I wanted to make sure I never ended up in a situation like that again. And I realized that I wanted to never drink again.

I had experience with AA and knew that it wasn't for me, so I set out to find a different approach. I found *This Naked Mind* in Barnes and Noble and devoured it. Reading it, I realized that not drinking feels so aligned with the person I want to be, with the work I want to do in the world. I'm getting ready to be a therapist. I want to be a safe presence. And it feels really good to be sober one hundred percent of the time. I've poured myself into reading, into learning, into my work. I want to build something, to have an impact on the world.

I was afraid that quitting alcohol would create distance between my best friend and me, because that's how we bonded. At first there was a little tension—I don't know if I imagined it or if she felt it too. She's never said she's done drinking, and I didn't want to push sobriety on her. But what's happened has been the most beautiful thing: she's almost completely quit, too. To me, that's so admirable. If she'd been ready to quit and I hadn't, I don't think I would've been able to quit with her. It's not something we've talked about much, so I don't know if it's the same for her, if alcohol had a grip on her the way it did on me. But I want to be clear on this point: It's not that I think I was addicted or even that I drank "too much." I just didn't want it in my life anymore. And that was enough reason to say, "No more." I didn't need to drag myself down to a dark place to justify giving up alcohol.

And it's a decision I'm so happy I've made. I had no idea how much I'd love this new way of living. Looking back, after the initial buzz, being drunk is uncomfortable. It didn't make me happy. I never want to do that again.

And now I know I'm not going to.

"Realizing my ideas come from my brain, not from the bottle, is empowering. It feels great to know I don't need alcohol at all, for anything. I am strong, happy, and whole just as I am."

—Annie Grace, *This Naked Mind*

WHEN THE EXCUSES FELT HOLLOW
Simon's Story

I always thought everyone drank enthusiastically. It's what we all do, right?

How wrong I was.

At forty-four years old, I thought my life was pretty good. I owned a successful business, had a lovely wife and teenage son, and didn't worry about money. Yet I never felt truly fulfilled. Something was missing—I knew it was—but I couldn't work out what. I just wasn't happy. I was turning into a sad, grumpy old man.

For twenty years, I got through at least a bottle of red wine every night—often two or more. It didn't bother me. I thought everyone drank like this. After all, people who had "problems" with alcohol drank until they fell apart . . . right? Their alcohol consumption wasn't like mine. I just drank to relax, to take the edge off the anxiety, for the taste, out of habit . . . the list of excuses went on.

I had suffered from anxiety since I was a teenager. I used to worry about things that often didn't even happen and would have meltdowns over minor things. I didn't realize at the time, but I was self-medicating my anxiety with alcohol. It made it go away for a few hours each evening, and it felt like relief.

But bit by bit, alcohol lost its magic. I was tiring of the daily ritual. Tiring of the hangovers, regrettable behavior, trembling hands . . . even of having a purple tongue! I was also worrying about the impact on my health. But I had no idea how to cut back. The idea of drinking less for even a single evening filled me with absolute dread. I had drunk every day for over twenty years. There was no way I could stop.

When I realized this, I started soul-searching. *Am I an alcoholic?* I opened up Google and filled out online questionnaires, and the answer always came back, blaring a warning, telling me my drinking was "dangerous" or "excessive." But I couldn't deal with those answers, so I put my mind at ease, making more excuses, reassuring myself that I didn't really have a problem.

There was no rock-bottom moment. I didn't crash my car while drunk or end up in jail through drinking. In fact, in some respects I wish I had—maybe it would have been a light-bulb moment that opened my eyes and forced me to change. Instead, I stayed stuck in my own self-made prison. So what did I do? I drank more to blot out the uncomfortable thoughts. The cycle went on daily for over five years.

I kept reassuring myself I didn't have a problem, but I knew that in truth I did. Slowly, those excuses felt more and more hollow. Searching for some action I could take, I joined a few sobriety groups on Facebook. I read their stories and envied their celebrations of how many days they'd been alcohol-free. Then I learned about a book called *This Naked Mind* and decided to read it.

I approached the book with an open mind, but I wasn't expecting a miracle. And yet it resonated so much with my own behaviors and habits that it was as if the book had been specifically written for me.

It deconstructed my beliefs about alcohol. My excuses fell away. Drinking *didn't* help me relax. It *didn't* ease my anxiety—maybe it shoved it aside for a few hours, but it always returned with a vengeance the next morning. I turned the last page and realized I was ready to stop. It wasn't that I *couldn't* have a drink. I simply *didn't want* one. Alcohol had started to feel insignificant to me.

That was the day I stopped drinking. I haven't looked back, and I will never drink again. The journey's been amazing. I'm happy and calm for the first time since childhood. It is all thanks to the inspiration of Annie's incredible work and the This Naked Mind community. I'm so happy and grateful for this new life, for the meaning and purpose, the joy and peace, the fulfillment that was missing for so long.

The biggest gift from my alcohol-free life was when my anxiety faded away after four or five months without drinking. The dark clouds of anxiety had hung over me for more than two decades, and suddenly it felt like those clouds were fading away and the sun was starting to shine into my life. It was an amazing feeling, and the great news is that the anxiety has never returned.

I found myself laughing and smiling again, engaging with my wife and son and genuinely enjoying the time we spent together. These days, I spend my time coaching and helping others. I have also become a supporter of the alcohol-free movement, and I work hard to spread the message about the huge benefits of an alcohol-free life.

So many incredible things have happened. They feel like gifts, and I cherish them dearly—and they are all a direct result of putting down the bottle and claiming control and power over my life.

"Drinking didn't make me funnier. How could it? When my brain functioned at a slower pace my wit was dulled."
—Annie Grace, *This Naked Mind*

I STARTED TO HEAL
Emma's Story

I'm a university lecturer in journalism. I worked for several years as a BBC TV news reporter and a news producer for the BBC news channel and a documentary channel. My father was a world-famous mathematician and vice-chancellor of a university.

I only mention all this because it's integral to the shame I felt over my drinking. When I found myself curled up in bed feeling sick yet again, a staccato refrain pounded in my mind in time with my headache: *I'm bright, successful, and highly educated. I have a degree from Oxford and a PhD. And I'm a drunk. How? How can I be all those things?*

Of course, *This Naked Mind* showed me just how easy it is to slide into the alcohol trap—that alcohol is an inherently addictive substance that no social status, professional success, or educational attainment protects us from.

In fact, for me, my career choices contributed to my drinking. As a journalist, heavy drinking was just part of the turf. I'd been drinking too much since I turned eighteen. In my heyday, I could drink two bottles of wine a day and suffer little hangover. In my twenties and thirties, I even managed to stay slim, attractive, and highly functional—though I did lose my driver's license for a year when I was in my mid-twenties. In hindsight, that should have been a blaring warning that something had gone wrong. But I didn't think too much about it. I started taking the bus and went on with my drinking.

Roll on twenty-five years, and my marriage fell apart. Never did I dream of blaming alcohol, but the truth was that there were three people in my marriage—me, John, and alcohol. And alcohol got more attention than anyone.

A little while later, I was living alone, and my dad died from a terrible cancer. I was devastated, and the bottle was the friend that got me through. Around that time, I was diagnosed with depression and was off work for six months. Again, this should have been an obvious warning bell, but I didn't hear it. Then, three years ago, out of the blue, my sister died of a brain aneurysm. She was only fifty-one and left behind two children, the youngest of whom was nine. I drank to oblivion to get through the pain.

A year later, I decided to try dating again and met an amazing man, who is now my partner. Graham had been in the music business, where alcohol flowed freely, and he'd given up drinking for fifteen years . . . but had picked it back up a year or so before we met. So we drank together, though the level at which I drank troubled him.

Then we went to France together, and I decided we should try all the wines of the region—an excuse for getting plastered with a thin veneer of respectability pasted over it. We drank and drank and drank . . . and then I fell, breaking my arm so badly I needed an emergency operation in France. The surgeons put a massive plate in, and the pain was horrific. After I got back to the UK, I needed a second operation. So much pain, so much lost time. Another warning sign, right?

But I still wasn't ready to heed the obvious. No, for me, it wasn't a dramatic incident that finally brought me to the point of being ready to quit. Instead, I quit because I started to heal.

Around the time I turned fifty-two—which meant I'd outlived my sister by a year—my arm finally got better. Those two things in conjunction got me ruminating on what I wanted out of the rest of my life.

And I realized that I didn't want alcohol to rule me. I found *This Naked Mind* and read it, and I've deconstructed my cognitive dissonance. It's all so clear to me now—what alcohol is, what it does. And I know I want no part of it. I'm buoyed up by my achievement. Graham has joined me as well. He's been so supportive, and he's as adamant as I am that our future will be alcohol-free.

I only wish my sister could see me now. She would be proud of me. But all I can do is seize life and live the rest of it well—for myself, for my sister, for Graham. And for me, living well means living alcohol-free. No more blowing past red flags, no more alcohol-induced accidents. Just freedom and healing and a fearless march into the future.

"When you are physically strong, you are on top of the world. You are present to enjoy the great moments in life."
—Annie Grace, *This Naked Mind*

VOTED "LEAST LIKELY TO EVER QUIT DRINKING"
Alex's Story

The phone rang. It was Lisa. I answered it, knowing I was going to need to help her calm down. Her second marriage wasn't going well—her husband was a heavy drinker, and she felt like she was being dragged even deeper into the booze-heavy lifestyle that had already taken so much from her. She'd been drinking more and more just to get a buzz. She used the alcohol to deal with life. Her teenagers were going wild. She was working hard during the week but binge drinking on the weekends to escape reality. She knew she had a problem, and so she was calling me, her long-time best friend, as she always did, to process her guilt and anxiety.

But I was wrong. This time, Lisa was different. "I've quit drinking," she said.

"You've what?" I asked.

"I'm serious. I've quit for good."

I was supportive—it was clear the alcohol hadn't been doing Lisa any favors—and a little bit jealous. If I was honest with myself, the alcohol hadn't been doing *me* any favors, either.

"I think you're going to stop too," she said. But she didn't press the issue or preach at me. She just waited patiently until I realized it.

Lisa and I met back in high school, through our parents. Our families both owned pubs and were close friends. Before we met, our stories paralleled in many ways—we practically grew up in our families' pubs, which meant alcohol was always normalized. I was plonked onto a bar for the first time at three days old.

We both ended up trying alcohol for the first time at a young age. My earliest memory of drinking was with my sister. I was five. My sister and I were playing, imitating our parents, and pouring drinks from the bar. Partway through, we decided to try some of the alcohol. This wasn't actually my first drink—when I was even younger, I'd had some red wine that had been left lying around the house—but it was the first one I remember. Lisa waited until she was a full six years old. She and another little friend started sneaking spiked punch at a family barbecue. The friend, age seven, ended up going home drunk.

In my house, there was always a party atmosphere that masked an acute pain beneath the surface—alcohol was taking hold of my father, leading to many arguments and a tense environment.

During our early teens, Lisa and I started to explore drinking regularly. We'd drink every weekend on the streets and get drunk in the back of the bus on the way to the under-eighteen disco. It felt like we came alive with each sip of booze. We were both shy, and alcohol made us confident, sociable, the life of the party. We actively encouraged and excused each other.

By our late teens, we were working for Lisa's mum in the pub. We were an amazing bar team. The customers loved buying us drinks, and we loved drinking them. And the party didn't stop when work ended. We'd go out to other bars that were open even later, or lock the doors when the pub shut down and carry on partying. We were known as the girls who could drink everyone under the table.

It was a crazy way to live, and we loved it. On several occasions, we got each other into trouble. Once, we went out and then came back to my house and decided—even after shots and three bottles of wine—we hadn't had enough and went back out again. Over the years, we've lost each other, left each other, used each other as excuses, and defended each other's disgusting behavior.

By our early thirties, we both had young children and had calmed down somewhat. Though we lived some distance apart, we still made time to see each other. We didn't go out as often, but when we did, we were back to our old habits. Our poor husbands dreaded our annual messy weekend in Dublin. We once tried to miss a flight home so we could stay and drink another day. Of course, even when we weren't getting smashed in another city, we still drank together. Many evenings, we hung out on videocalls, chatting and drinking wine.

"This is great!" I said once. "It's our night out, but in."

Of course, we embraced mummy wine culture—led the pack, even. But we knew it had a dark side. Though we were functional—we held down good jobs, families, and friendships—we called each other every weekend, crying and ashamed. Over the years, we both went through marriage breakdowns and lost our fathers and a mutual friend to alcohol. And still, we enabled each other. We were each other's metaphorical worst enemy and best friend at the same time.

I worked a lot and rarely drank on the weekdays, but I was always looking forward to Friday. Every Friday and Saturday, I'd drink a bottle or two of red wine in the house. I did try to quit after an incident in which I threw a sandwich at my husband's head because he was going out to the pub and I had to stay in, and then I drank myself into a stupor alone in the house. For a while, I stopped because I believed he would leave me. Then I found out I was pregnant, which made it easy to not drink. Unfortunately, I lost the baby at three months and went straight to the pub and drank. This went on for another ten months. I was miserable, bitter, angry, and resentful when I was drunk, which was often.

And then Lisa called to tell me she'd quit drinking and that she thought I would quit too.

After watching her thrive for almost a year, I decided enough was enough and that I was ready to have my last drink. Lisa joined me for the occasion. Both of us knew we would never drink again—and our horrific hangovers the next day sealed the deal.

Together, we started to discuss the benefits of sobriety, and she handed me *This Naked Mind*. After reading it, I knew really and truly that I was done for good. That alcohol hadn't done anything positive for me, and I wanted to not only be free but to dedicate my life to helping people uncover the truth.

Our friends have been curious—we would have been voted "least likely to ever quit drinking"—and through conversations with them, we've helped several of them become sober, including Lisa's mum, my sister, and some old school friends. What a rewarding feeling! Now we're active on social media and are undertaking a project to give workplace presentations on health and wellbeing—including the truth about alcohol. We've studied coaching and mentoring, and we are using our self-education to support others in this most meaningful of journeys—the sober revolution!

"On the beach with an excellent book, enjoying the sun and the breeze off the ocean, without a care in the world, I am fully relaxed. Alcohol can't improve that feeling."
—Annie Grace, *This Naked Mind*

FROM DRINKING TO FIT IN TO DRINKING TO GET BY
Amanda's Story

It's time I'm honest. It's time I tell the truth. It's time I find the real me and not the person I became when I was trying so hard to fit in.

My first sip of alcohol happened the summer before senior year of high school. My older sister had hidden vodka in a water bottle, and after a long summer shift of scooping ice cream in eighty-five-degree heat, I was thirsty. I took a giant sip and sputtered as the liquor burned all the way down my throat. My sister laughed hysterically when she realized my mistake.

The next time I drank was with my boyfriend's friend—he assured me it was safe and would make me better prepared for college. The time after that was at a party after I'd broken up with my boyfriend. This time, I was ready to experience my full potential as a drinker and a party girl. I threw caution to the wind, played strip pong, and hooked up with a guy I barely knew. Things got worse from there.

Deep down, I didn't want to go to college. I didn't want to struggle to be cool or work to fit in. I dreaded being the girl without a "crew." So shortly after starting classes, I joined a sorority. It wasn't one of the sadistic ones you read about, but alcohol did flow like water. Plus, the frat guys were always welcoming to a decent-looking girl who was down to party. By this point, I was drinking to fit in.

Getting mono, taking Plan B, racking up debt, and enduring too many hangovers to count weren't letters of shame—they were great stories to tell, awesome ways to win at "never have I ever." Thank goodness I still passed my classes, but I didn't live up to my academic potential. That's one of my greatest regrets—that I drank instead of soaking up all the knowledge that was available to me. But I was still so concerned about fitting in, and I found popularity as a party girl. Everyone said a party was better if I was there. People begged me to host their pre-games and costume parties. How could a little nobody like me give up on all that?

About three-quarters of the way through college, I reunited with my high school boyfriend. While drinking had never been part of our high school relationship, it was the center of our college relationship—after all, it was college! When would we ever get to live like this again? Thursday through Tuesday we knew how to get the cheapest booze—Wednesday was the day we "took off to recover." It was exhausting, and I even relapsed into mono again—not something that usually happens. Still, it never occurred to me to stop drinking.

Post-graduation, I was relieved to get a job near my boyfriend, out of state. My parents—practicing Catholics—didn't know the extent of my drinking, and I planned to keep it that way. The party life continued, but it looked more like a solo dinner party and a bottle of cheap wine after a long, stressful day of teaching. I was tired and constantly hungover but functional and even professionally successful. When I did hang out with friends, it was usually with my boyfriend's coworkers, who loved to drink.

I wasn't drinking to fit in anymore—I was drinking just to get by. Fast-forward three years. My boyfriend and I got married and bought a house. Then, I found out I was pregnant, while holding a glass of good wine in my hand. Sadly, I poured it down the sink. It horrifies me to write this, but I was sadder about not being able to drink than I was happy about the pregnancy.

Being pregnant was rough. I had hyperemesis gravidarum, likely as a result of my wine and carb-forward diet. I lost thirty pounds and had to quit my job. Worse, I was startled to realize how few people wanted to hang out with me and my growing belly—all our friends were heavy drinkers. I felt lost, outcast.

Shortly after the baby was born, we sold our house and moved to another state, seven hundred miles away. The cost of living was lower, and that meant we could afford for me to stay home with the baby. Then we got pregnant again, only six months after our move, and I was utterly isolated and alone. We lived in a shoebox apartment with no space, and my every waking moment was occupied by a toddler and a colicky newborn. I had no world to retreat to, except alcohol. I just had to keep it under control. As long as I didn't drink *too* much, I thought I could still take good care of my kids. I even believed alcohol made me a better mother—when I didn't drink, I was moody and sad, but when I did drink, I was tired but calm.

My husband and I realized we were both unhappy living so far from our hometown, so we decided to move back less than two years later. I rejoiced! At last, I'd be free. I'd have help with the kids. My life was finally everything I'd wanted: a loving husband, kids, family, friends, and my home church.

By this point, I was firmly addicted to alcohol. A drink with dinner could turn into a whole bottle. Parties with my family were landmines—alcohol was always served, but there was a sense of shame about actually drinking too much. My parents are loving, generous people, but they have high standards that were hard for me to navigate with my addiction. I felt pressure: be the life of the party, but don't overdo it.

At my sister's house, I finally overdid it. The drunk version of myself flipped the bird in front of my horrified parents. At the time, I was joking and thought it was hilarious. It would have been acceptable at a party in college, or even at my sister's if my parents and aunt weren't in attendance. But I wasn't able to read the dynamics of the room and control my behavior.

That set off my journey of questioning my relationship with alcohol. My mother accused me of losing control. Had I? Had I passed that fine line between moderation and free-for-all? I read every book I could and finally found *This Naked Mind*.

I opened the book, wondering: Do I have alcoholism or not? But as I read, I realized it was the wrong question. I should have been asking, *Is alcohol serving me well? Am I living with truth and integrity? Am I happy with this? Is this how I want to live each week?*

My priorities had shifted in the years since I began drinking. My friendships all had nothing to do with alcohol. I did drink a lot with my husband, so I was apprehensive about what our marriage would look like if I wasn't drinking, but he was totally supportive of my quitting. Also, I wanted more kids, but the idea of parenting three or four on crappy, alcohol-fueled sleep was utterly exhausting. Just imagining it makes me ready for a nap. I knew that if I chose alcohol, I'd be prioritizing it over the beautiful babies I felt so ready to welcome. Would I let a wine habit rob me of my deepest desires? For a long time, I let it steal so much from me. It made me a subpar mom. I'm a preschool teacher and I love children; my life centers around them. Yet with my own children, I snapped and yelled because I was too tired or too hungover to really play.

I had my final drink at my husband's friend's beach wedding. Buzzed but not drunk, I was feeling beautiful and in control. But in the heat, I got dehydrated and turned into a sweaty, out-of-control mess. Finally, after a friend of a friend's husband hit on me at the bar, my drunk brain had a moment of clarity. I found my husband and said, "I've had enough."

He thought I'd meant enough for the night and took me back

to the hotel, ignoring my ramblings about that idiot jerk and his oblivious wife. He gave me water and tucked me in. The next day, he drove the whole six hours back home, listening to me retch in the back seat. It was a hangover for the books. And I knew that the subpar, thick, warm, too-sweet glass of red wine had been my last.

I promised myself and my husband that I wouldn't be wasting any more days hungover in bed. Though I haven't sat down to have a conversation with my kids yet—they're still very young—I know I have to be proactive to counter the brainwashing they'll be exposed to from the culture. Now, wrapped into my desire to be a great mommy is the knowledge that I need to be an informative one. My children will know that alcohol is a poison and how to avoid it.

Not drinking means that I'm rediscovering the person I really am, the person I gave up to fit in and be popular. And I like myself—my *real* self—better than I ever did as a college party girl or a wine-o'clock young mom.

"A single, strong choice made with all your brain liberates you from willpower."
—Annie Grace, *This Naked Mind*

I WASN'T IN CONTROL
Christine's Story

For months, I'd been secretly questioning my drinking. My grandfather, uncle, and brother had their lives destroyed by alcohol. The rest of us all believed it was because of the "defective gene" that causes alcoholism. I felt sorry for them—that they had lost control of their drinking and let it ruin their lives. I had no idea, then, that alcohol is not something you can control.

It's addictive and, given time and the right circumstances, it will take over your life. I thought (like most of society) that if you didn't have that "alcoholic gene" (or as epigenetics states, have it "turned on"), you were safe and could drink "moderately" or "responsibly." This, of course, was such a relief to me since I loved my wine. I loved what I believed it did for me—like helping me enjoy parties or allowing me to relax after long workdays—yet in the back of my mind, I always knew I needed to be careful because "alcoholism runs in the family."

I had an eating disorder for many years. I tried to control it by exercising often and eating only certain foods. I was always focused on it and never felt I could "let my guard down" around food. I hated social events where I knew there would be lots of food. After restricting myself for so long, I would end up giving in and eating everything I normally wouldn't allow myself to.

On the outside, I looked very fit and always had an outgoing personality, so people never knew my inner struggle with food. Often, I received compliments about my fitness, yet I never felt free inside or happy with myself. Finally, I quit my job at a gym to be a housewife and allowed myself to just stop controlling everything. In one year, I gained over thirty pounds.

For the first time in years, I was eating whatever I wanted and accepting and loving myself just as I was. So far, so good. Then my drinking increased, and although I wanted to start taking better care of myself again (just not fanatically), alcohol took away my motivation to do anything. All I thought about was when I could drink again—then I felt bad about drinking! The cognitive dissonance was driving me crazy!

There came a point where I was drinking more than I wanted to and getting less joy out of it. Instead of stopping after the buzz of a glass or two of wine and enjoying the soft edges it put around everything, I craved more. I told myself I liked how it made me slow down and relax. I was enjoying setting up our new house and working on the property.

When I worked at the gym, I only drank in the evening. Having all this time on my hands, I started drinking earlier and earlier. I even remember reading that one of the signs of alcohol abuse is drinking often before noon. I would tell myself, "Well, you can wait until noon, so you must not have a problem." Yet, I wondered (in brief moments on and off) if I was fooling myself.

Once all my daily work was done, I'd feel bored and full of energy that I didn't know what to do with. Having some wine helped me slow down and bear the boredom. Soon enough, I was having my first one at eleven in the morning. Then it turned into another and another, until I had finished a whole bottle by the time my husband got home from work. At that point, I was tired and cranky and wanted to get through dinner so I could collapse into bed. I lost interest in watching TV together or talking to him about things. Sadly, I was always worried about how much I was drinking and hoping it wasn't affecting my liver or health.

My tolerance was such that I never really felt drunk and seemed to be able to function well while drinking. I would have some wine and mow the lawn or do other chores. For the longest time, I hated hard liquor and never "acquired the taste" for beer. While on a tour of Scotland for two months, I learned to really like the taste of Scotch whiskey and loved touring the distilleries and tasting the many different kinds of Scotch in all the pubs. I fell prey to all the hype most people believe: *it helps you have fun and enjoy yourself; everyone does it, so don't worry—you're in control; it tastes so good; it looks great in those beautiful bottles; it smells wonderful; it enhances your dinner or special occasion; it's calming and relaxing; it's the social thing to do.*

Never did I believe I would reach the point where I knew I was not in control of alcohol anymore—it controlled me! I kept all my concerns to myself for fear of being judged, and I worried that my husband (who enjoyed his nightly beer) was looking at me like I had a problem, like he had to worry about me. I was afraid of the label "alcoholic" and dreaded the thought of going to AA meetings for the rest of my life, living without alcohol but wanting it all the time. I didn't want to become a "dry drunk," or someone who gives up alcohol but then becomes miserable and obsessed with not drinking!

At first, I promised myself that I would have just one or two in the afternoon, but then that bottle would call for my attention, and I would go to the fridge and pour "just a little more." After all, if a little is good, more will be better, right? The alcohol was driving me. When I went to bed, I'd lie there so afraid that I couldn't stop and worried about how much more I would end up drinking if I carried on like this.

So, I decided (more than once) that I just couldn't drink at all, and I'd be able to go a few days without drinking. Then something would happen or a situation where I always enjoyed drinking would come up, and I'd buy a bottle of my favorite white wine, telling myself, "You've been able to stop for a few days, and you didn't have withdrawals, so you're obviously not addicted."

I would go through that bottle in one day and start planning when to buy the next one. I worried about the money I spent, so I started buying the cheaper bottles. I was totally mentally dependent on alcohol.

I finally decided to let my husband know about my struggles, downplaying them by asking for his support to stop drinking because I no longer enjoyed how it made me feel. I couldn't let him know how worried I was or how much I was drinking, because I feared he would see me as weak or an alcoholic. I wanted to be in control of quitting and not be labeled. He loves me very much and has always been supportive of me in everything (my fears were all in my own head). So, I told him I wanted to quit, not letting him know the times I had already tried and failed, and asked if I could just "check in with him" daily to let him know how I was doing and get his support if I was tempted to buy wine.

Doing this did help because I felt so relieved that he knew I wanted to quit. Being accountable to him meant I could no longer drink at home. But inside, my fear of being an alcoholic was still there, and I had no idea if I could keep it up or even enjoy my life without booze. I felt sad, like I was losing a friend and giving up the enjoyment and happiness I got from drinking. Little did I know, these are all lies, and realizing that would free me from wanting to drink!

A few days after I stopped drinking, my husband told me he'd bought a book I might enjoy reading, called *This Naked Mind: Control Alcohol*.

At first, I thought, *Ugh, it's probably a book about giving up alcohol and how bad it is for me and how I will just have to live without it if I don't want to end up with physical problems. Yuck!*

It felt like I was going to have to learn all this stuff I would hate and then have to practice things that would take work. Worse, that I'd be consumed with *not drinking* and have to make a lot of lifestyle changes by force and out of fear.

I remember thinking, *Well, he bought it to be helpful, and I don't want to not read it, so I'll read a bit and then return it and tell him I just want to do it on my own.*

I'd start to read it, then put it down for a while. Then I'd feel guilty, like I should give it a chance (before returning it). So, I picked it up again. This time, as I read, something began to click with me. I started to like what I was reading, and it all made perfect sense! Maybe I could be free!

I got very excited as I realized I wasn't sick or weak. No, I didn't have an alcoholic gene or an addictive personality. I was just addicted to alcohol because it's an extremely addictive drug. Most importantly, I could decide to stop once I learned the truth.

To know that I am in control of alcohol and not the other way around is amazing. Now I know the truth—alcohol does nothing for me that I can't do for myself. I can relax and be social without it! I can go out to dinner and not have wine! It's a poison, and why would I ever want to poison myself? It just makes me tired and cranky and hungry.

I have found such joy in living each day, handling whatever comes (good or bad) and knowing I don't need alcohol to get me through. The confidence I feel has inspired me to start cooking and baking healthy, delicious food. My days are now filled with doing things I *want* to do. I have the energy and desire I lost while drinking to do the things I love.

I have wonderful grandchildren and a new baby grandson. I feel great joy in being able to watch him while his mom works part-time. When I was drinking, I'd enjoy being with them but had to have some wine beforehand. And if I couldn't, I'd be preoccupied during our time together, wondering when I could leave and have some wine.

My husband and I celebrated his birthday recently by going to dinner with my son and daughter-in-law, and I enjoyed the meal and their company without wanting any alcohol. I have so much more clarity, contentment, and peace. Even when things go really wrong, I am calm and handle it without thinking I need to drink to cope. I will be turning sixty-two next week, but I feel like I'm decades younger.

Now I don't have to use willpower to not drink, because I no longer *want* to drink! Before, when I'd try to quit, I felt I was giving up something that really helped me mentally but that I knew wasn't good for me anymore. So it was a constant battle in my head. Now that I know the truth, that alcohol did nothing for me, I no longer want it. I'm thrilled to have found out that I really don't need it. Today, I am loving life and all the new things I am capable of doing!

I'm exercising again, but in ways that I enjoy. Not because I have to, but because I feel good when I do. Most poignantly, for many years, I've had the desire to help others and be a motivational speaker. I was involved with two Christian cults, married three times—twice to abusive men—and worked as a corrections officer in a men's prison for five years. I worked for six years with the destitute in South Africa, where my only son was born. I had to flee the country with him. I put myself through college as a single mother, got off welfare, became a social worker, overcame bulimia and anorexia, and now I've been freed from addiction too!

In recent years, alcohol had taken away any desire to fulfill my purpose in life, and I wasn't taking any steps toward that motivational speaking career. Now, thanks to *This Naked Mind* and my newfound freedom, I have that dream back in full force, and nothing will stop me now.

"I often notice people who aren't drinking or are drinking so little you can tell it's for show. They are enjoying the atmosphere, laughing, and talking with friends. They are not controlled by alcohol—they seem at peace and truly happy."

—Annie Grace, *This Naked Mind*

DO YOU REMEMBER?
Melissa's Story

This year has been a time of big change. As I neared forty, I quit my job of seventeen years and started studying full-time at university to be a primary school teacher. I also finally made the decision to stop drinking alcohol.

If someone had told me two years ago that I'd be in this situation, I wouldn't have believed them in a million years. I never thought it would be possible for me to go alcohol-free and enjoy it—much less to feel like it's the best decision I've ever made. Alcohol has been a significant part of my adulthood. Even though I hated the shame and the hangovers, I thought it was an essential part of being social.

It's funny when I say that, because my parents didn't really drink when I was a child. I've never once seen them drink to excess. They had me later in life—my dad was forty-seven and my mom was thirty-seven—and I've been told my dad used to love to drink. From the stories I've heard, he was a happy drinker but tended to have a few too many beers after work or on Saturday afternoon in the backyard.

I have the vaguest memory of him sitting under a tree with an afternoon beer. But when I was quite small, he had a health scare.

The doctors told him to stop drinking for six months. Once the six months were up, he never picked it up again. He's now eighty-eight, fit, healthy, and loving life. He hasn't had a drink in nearly forty years and is one of my inspirations.

And still, despite that role model, I got sucked into the alcohol trap.

When I was around fifteen, I went on vacation with a friend whose parents liked drinking. They returned to the holiday house late one night, both obviously drunk. I'd never seen a drunk person before, and I was shocked and confused—even a bit scared—by their behavior. It was nothing bad. They were just laughing and making silly jokes. But I didn't really know what it meant to be drunk. I'd never had much interest in alcohol.

A couple years later, my friends and I started going to parties on the weekends. My friends wanted to drink, so we would talk a friend's mum into buying us a hip flask of Jim Beam to share between the three of us—we told her it was for thirty people, of course. We never really got drunk on it, though, just a bit tipsy. We were too scared to ever drink it all.

Right after high school, I went to a party and drank Polish vodka. It tasted like rocket fuel, but my friends were there, and so were my then-boyfriend and his friends. So I persisted, unaware of how powerful it was. That night, I got extremely drunk and vomited at my friend's house. I believe that was the first time I blacked out, though I didn't realize at the time that's what had happened.

Despite the next day's hangover, that was the real start of my next two decades of drinking. My friends and I partied regularly all throughout our twenties, and less frequently into our late thirties. I loved to dance. I loved my friends. I loved having fun. And I loved to drink when I did all of those things.

In those early years, we'd go out Thursday, Friday, and Saturday nights and drink to excess. I never consciously thought, "Oh, let's go get hammered tonight," but that was always what happened. Once I started drinking, I got out of control really quickly. The night would take on a life of its own. And sometimes that would happen before we even started partying—we would pre-drink to save money. By the time I left the house, I was often already drunk. I was very lucky that nothing terrible happened to me during those years, though there are a few instances of casual sex that I regret and still feel shame about.

In some ways, I got off easy because I didn't like drinking alone. I was purely a social drinker. So even though I got drunk every weekend, often to the point of blacking out, that kept me from escalating to daily drinking. Another dynamic that helped keep me grounded was a decrease in my partying whenever I was in a relationship—at least if my boyfriend didn't drink a lot. Though if I was dating a guy who liked to party too much . . . then it could be game on.

Throughout these years, in the back of my mind I knew there was something wrong with my relationship with alcohol. I don't think I drank differently than anyone else, but it seemed to affect me differently. I was much more prone to blackouts than my friends, and when I got too drunk, I lost control of what I was doing and saying, which is such a horrible feeling.

"Do you remember what you did last night?"

It was my least favorite question after a night of drinking. Because too often, I didn't. My behavior wasn't usually spectacularly bad, but I'd say stuff I'd never say sober and do things I wished I hadn't. I put up with that shame and anxiety for a long time because I didn't feel like I could abstain in those environments, and I loved going out with my friends.

At the age of thirty-five, after a particularly drunken night at my fitness club's mid-year party, I decided to address my drinking. I've always been a fit and healthy person, and at my gym, people trained hard and partied hard. At this particular party, I blacked out and uncharacteristically told my sister to "fuck off" when she tried to get me to go home.

The next day, she had a serious conversation with me about my drinking. She was the first—and only—person to ever talk to me about it. Looking back, I'm extremely grateful for her concern. At the time, I knew she was doing it because she cared, but I wasn't quite sure how to fix my problem. Still, I decided to try.

First, I went to a psychologist. Therapy was comforting and helpful in many ways, but I didn't stop drinking. I tried to quit for three months, but three months felt like an eternity. The idea of quitting paralyzed me with fear, and my journey stopped before it ever really started. So I decided to try out moderation.

I made a new rule: no more than four drinks when going out. Of course, by the fourth drink, I was already Drunk Melissa, and Drunk Melissa will just keep on drinking. I was successful on some nights, but I had to be strict and conscious about it, which was draining. I got so tired of always having to think about it. And sometimes, I'd end up having ten drinks anyway and wake up with a pounding hangover and memory loss.

After a year of moderating with the barest minimum of success, I decided I was better and stopped paying attention. My sister had gotten off my back because she hadn't witnessed my worst incidents.

By this time, I was still going out to party regularly—not every weekend, but still a couple times a month. My blackout episodes were happening less frequently, once a month or once every two months. After all these years, I'd pretty much trained myself to not say or do anything stupid—most of the time. But I was still sometimes making a fool of myself, and at my age, the shame and embarrassment was awful. The hangovers had gotten worse, too, and could last four or five days.

As I drew closer and closer to my fortieth birthday, I didn't want to behave in this manner anymore. I couldn't take the hangovers. What if I blacked out and woke up to find I'd done something horrendous? What if I blacked out and just didn't wake up? I didn't want to do that to my family or myself.

The price of partying had become too high. Alcohol had stripped me of everything I was. When I was drunk, I didn't know myself anymore. I didn't recognize myself. And deep down, I knew I either had to stop of my own accord, or something out of my control would make me stop.

Finally, I woke up one morning with a brutal hangover and had to piece together what had happened during the last three hours of the night by looking at my Uber receipts. I'd been out with people I didn't know very well, so they had no responsibility to take care of me. Which should be fine. I'm an adult. I shouldn't need someone to take care of me. But I also knew this hadn't been a safe situation. Those questions played over in my mind again.

What if I black out and wake up to find I've done something horrendous? What if I black out and just don't wake up?

That was it. I was done. I decided I couldn't drink anymore—but there was a new element that hadn't been there when I'd gone to therapy to sort out my drinking. For the first time, I didn't *want* to drink anymore.

At this point, I discovered *This Naked Mind* and started reading it, and it was like all the stars had aligned. What did I have to lose? I knew alcohol was taking and taking from me and not giving anything back.

So I stopped drinking. And it's been really, really amazing, one of the best decisions I've ever made.

I still go out with my friends and socialize and dance, but I'm happy doing those things alcohol-free. From my fortieth birthday, to a pub crawl with friends, to vacation—I've done all these things that I hadn't imagined would be fun sober. And it's been great!

In the beginning, I'd pretend to drink—I'd get a soda water and lime and let people assume there was vodka in it. To tell you the truth, it took them a long time to notice. Some of my friends said,

"Oh, no fun! You've got to have a drink!" But I was just as fun to be with when sober—after all, they'd been partying with me and hadn't realized I wasn't drinking.

So, I think those negative reactions aren't really about me and my decision. My not-drinking is holding up a mirror to them and their behavior. Alcohol isn't a common denominator for us anymore.

Really, not drinking makes everything *more* fun because I can dance and hang out with my friends and *keep those memories*. I don't lose pieces of those nights to blackouts. And really, when I blacked out, I lost the whole night. Even if there were only a few hours I couldn't remember, those memory gaps ruined the entire thing for me because I was so stressed out about what I might have said or done. If I blacked out at all, I didn't want to think about that night again. Now, I get to enjoy the night *and* the memory.

But I don't want to make it sound like my friends haven't been supportive, because most of them really have been. The ones who are uncomfortable with it have been in the minority. I think most of my friends are amazed, in a good way, that it's even possible. Just last week, one of them told me, "I think you've made the best decision for yourself."

And my family's really been great. Whenever my dad hears I'm going out, he says, "Melissa, don't drink now, come on."

I smile and tell him that it's OK, that I'm not going to drink. And I know it's true, because sometimes I cannot believe how lucky I am to be alcohol-free. I'm so excited to continue this journey, to make—and keep—new memories, to take control as I move into this next stage of my life. The world feels fresh and new. I have so much more clarity about who I am, what I enjoy, and how I want to live my life. And I'm *especially* happy to know I won't have to deal with another hangover or blackout ever again.

"*Alcohol is addictive because you wind up worse off after each drink. And you mistakenly believe that another drink will bring you back up. It's the problem and the solution at the same time. It's the chicken and the egg. It's a cycle. And you can break it if you choose.*"

—Annie Grace, *The Alcohol Experiment*

A LIFE-GIVING HEALTH JOURNEY
Harvey's Story

I come from a strict, no-drinking family. For part of my childhood, I was raised in the Mormon church, which prohibits all alcohol. Though alcohol was never in the house, I did have an uncle who would drive from San Antonio to California in his sports car and show off, and he drank—a ton. To my childhood self, he was the coolest person I could imagine. In addition, I got some early lessons from Hollywood—I idolized the cocktails they made in *Bewitched*. To me, it seemed like alcohol was a cool thing that I'd be able to drink when I was an adult.

My mom died of cancer when I was four, and my father was killed by a drunk driver when I was seven. My older sister and brother walked in the door and said, "Dad's dead, and you're coming with us." That was it. My childhood life, as I knew it, was over, and I was taken abruptly from my mountain home.

I was fortunate to be raised by my sister, but I always felt sort of left out. Throughout my childhood, I built up a lot of resentment. The day I turned eighteen, I packed up my car and moved out. After that, I pretty much drank every day for my whole life. It was the center of my social life and the way I coped with my emotions. I reveled in my drinking time with friends. It wasn't that I judged people who didn't drink, but I felt sorry for them—like they were missing out.

I sort of fell into the restaurant business as a way of putting myself through college. I really liked the social atmosphere and discovered I was a good waiter, so I worked my way up in the industry. Eventually, I became a chef and then started my own catering business in Los Angeles in the mid-1990s.

Over the years, my career had become unsatisfying. It was successful—I had good clients and made a good living, but I wanted more. I was also feeling sick all the time—I was drinking too much and my eating habits were terrible. My digestive system wasn't working. The liver tests were giving me bad news. I was feeling dissatisfied in general from a spiritual standpoint, and I started looking for something different.

As I was searching for a new career and better health, someone introduced me to a network marketing wellness company with a nutrition component. The entrepreneur in me was curious, and I decided to check it out. I sold the products and began a Facebook support group where people who bought my products could get healthy recipes. I dove into learning about nutrition, and the group took off, growing to fifteen hundred members. People called me a health guru. So, I evaluated my authenticity in this situation.

If I'm going to represent a health product, I really need to accelerate this health thing, I thought. I started consciously eating better and drinking less, and I got a lot healthier just from my diet—but I still wasn't taking the alcohol particularly seriously.

One of my drinking buddies invited me to join his Dry January group. It was an interesting challenge—I'd never thought of stopping before. I mean, I'd evaluated my drinking over the years, but whenever I'd asked any of my friends if they thought I had a problem, they'd reassured me I was just fine. Because in our alcohol-drenched culture, no one has an alcohol problem unless they're a special person with a special problem, and that means they're so out of control that they hit rock bottom. Since I wasn't living on the streets, my friends thought I was doing great. So, when my buddy invited me to do Dry January, I took it as a challenge, even though it was kind of a scary prospect.

I'm the sort of person who takes things head-on and does nothing by half measure, so I aced Dry January and outlasted everyone else in the group. But that only emboldened me to drink more—if I could go a whole month without drinking, that clearly meant I didn't need to be careful with alcohol.

Another year went by, and we decided to do Dry January again. But this time, I couldn't stop drinking. I kept putting it off, saying every Monday that I'd start the next weekend. Finally, I woke up one Monday and said, "This is a serious problem."

So, I dragged myself to an AA meeting. While AA didn't end up working for me, I have to give it kudos because I don't know if I would have started on this journey without it. But while I was in AA, I was in a spiral—quit, relapse, feel self-loathing, quit again, repeat.

I was sitting at my computer one day, looking at social media, when Annie Grace popped up on my screen. She was talking about *This Naked Mind*, and I thought, *This sounds really interesting*.

Something deep inside me responded to the message of the book. I knew there had to be a better, more efficient way to get control of my drinking. A couple weeks later, after another relapse, I downloaded the book and devoured it in two and a half days. It completely changed my life and spoke to me on so many levels. It made sense from a scientific perspective—the studies and the statistics worked for me. Through reading the book, I healed my relationship with alcohol, and that opened up a whole new world. The inner athlete in me came out, the inner nerd came out. I've been studying, expanding my credentials, getting formal training as a nutritionist.

Now I use the principles that I learned in the book in my nutrition practice, because a lot of the same principles of neuroscience apply to food. I was able to so completely rewire my brain that I can drink alcohol in moderation, and it doesn't set me back. However, as I've dived deeper into my nutritional training, I've gotten to the point where I'm not interested in moderating. I don't want to drink at all because alcohol is so unhealthy. It's a total negative in terms of nutrition, and I don't want to put something like that in my body anymore. If my mission is to be healthier and to help other people be healthier, having a drink is acting against my mission. It's like saying I want to drive from here to Salt Lake City, and then I start throwing boulders in front of the car. Alcohol is bad for your digestion, your liver, your nervous system, your hormones. It contributes to type 2 diabetes, screws up carbohydrate metabolism, impairs absorption of vitamins and minerals, and suppresses the immune system.

I want to move my body forward on a health continuum at all times. That was my mantra. Finally, when I came to terms with leaving moderate drinking behind, I said, "I only put things in my body that are life-giving. That's it." That's true for alcohol, as well as things like processed sugar. And I'm going to help more people in a more powerful way if I stay true to that and don't drink at all. The world doesn't need another person to conform to a way of life that's destroying society. It needs people to take a stand. So, I'm going to take that stand, representing a different way of life. I hope that inspires my clients and helps everyone I interact with live a healthier life.

"When you make a decision that you're not a drinker anymore, that's it. You're free from the hamster wheel. Alcohol no longer has a hold over you because you are of one mind. Your conscious and subconscious want the same thing. How cool is that?"

—Annie Grace, *The Alcohol Experiment*

SENDING MY LIVER ON HOLIDAY
Marietta's Story

I had my first glass of wine when I was about ten, though my aunt had given me a spiked egg punch when I was even younger. I was born in the sixties in Holland, when cultural norms were beginning to loosen up and there were fewer boundaries. My parents tried to be very modern and tolerant, and so they allowed us to have an occasional glass of wine at Christmas or when they threw parties.

The alcohol made me giggle. Like any ten-year-old, I found it exciting to get to join the adults, but the wine itself drew me in too. I was very shy and insecure back then. However, when I had a glass of wine or two, all of a sudden, I wasn't shy anymore. I could make people laugh, and I would laugh with them.

When I was fifteen, I dated an older boy who drank a lot of beer. I had to attend classes and do my homework, so I didn't drink during the week. But on the weekends, I drank with my boyfriend and his friends, often until I got sick. More than once, I got home trying to hide my drunkenness from my parents as I made it to bed, only to have the world start spinning until I threw up. One time, I was too drunk to reach the loo, so I threw up in the washbasin and was unable to clean it up. My mom was cross with me the next morning—not because I'd been drunk, but because I'd left vomit in the washbasin.

Now, I think, *Thank God for that*, because if I hadn't thrown up, I might have had severe alcohol poisoning. My body got sick to protect me from all the beer. At this time, I was still incredibly shy, and I think that's the reason I drank so much. Even then, I knew it was too much and wanted to cut back. On occasion, I told myself that I wouldn't have any alcohol that weekend, that I'd stick to soda or fruit juice, but I never did. I always ended up drinking with the boys.

When I went to university at age eighteen, I fell in love with a guy who drank a lot. I thought I could make him happy and that if he was happy, he wouldn't drink so much. You can imagine how that turned out. Instead of helping him cut back, I ended up drinking with him. We got married and had children, and even though we'd been drinking in large quantities every night, I didn't have a problem stopping when I was pregnant or breastfeeding. Taking the break was easy because I knew what I was doing it for.

The marriage didn't work out—he was an abusive narcissist, and the relationship was toxic. For a while afterward, I dealt with PTSD and didn't know how to handle it. In the '90s, no one was talking about narcissistic abuse, and I lacked the understanding and the tools to cope with what had happened to me. I drank to get through those days, to ease the flashbacks and panic. Of course, it helped—I got so numb I didn't feel anything anymore.

I was a teacher then, and I'd go to school hungover. Imagine managing difficult classrooms with a pounding headache and nausea—I don't know how I did it over and over again. After some time, I met the man who is now my husband of more than twenty years. He hardly drank, and I found that attractive—he was always himself. He never became a different person. To this day, I've never seen him drunk.

We got together, and I was quite happy. He was so stable that

I was able to start healing from the PTSD and could handle the flashbacks better. Still, I was quite insecure, and I brought alcohol into our relationship. We ended up sharing a bottle—sometimes more—almost every night. This is embarrassing to admit, but I was so desperate to get enough wine that I topped off my glass when he went to the loo. That way I could make sure I got more than my share of the bottle.

After a stressful situation with my ex-husband, I realized that I had to be sober for my children. I started to take alcohol breaks. I went to an AA meeting, where they did the first of the twelve steps. The attendees each told their story of their powerlessness with alcohol, how they'd lost all control. I felt like I didn't belong there because I wasn't out of control. I used alcohol to ease my shyness and quiet my demons, but I never had cravings during work hours, never had shakes, never had a blackout.

I'm not that bad, I concluded. After a break of three or four months, I'd forgotten why I'd even stopped. *Maybe I could pick it back up again,* I thought. *I'll stick to just a glass or two at a time.* Three weeks later, I found myself drinking at the same level I'd been at before I stopped.

This turned into a pattern that lasted years. Whenever I decided to go on a break, I announced it in a sort of ironic way: "I'm sending my liver on holiday." The holiday reliably lasted three or four months, and then I'd start drinking again. Through this process, however, I discovered that I had a lot of friends and colleagues who were thinking about their relationships with alcohol and weren't comfortable with how much they were drinking. They were often intrigued by the fact that I was taking a break, and sometimes they'd even say that it was something they wanted to do too. It wasn't just me, and it wasn't just the people in that AA meeting. Alcohol seemed to have a troubling effect on so many of my acquaintances.

Then, after more than ten years of this, my mother and brother came to stay with us. My brother had had a huge drinking problem, and he'd quit alcohol altogether two years earlier. So I decided that I was going to support him by not drinking over Christmas, and I took another break. But something had shifted in me, and I wondered if I could make the break permanent like my brother had. Could I keep it up and not continue the cycle of starting back at it after two or three months?

I searched the web and found the website and YouTube channel for This Naked Mind. It gave me a whole new way of looking at alcohol. When I think back on all my embarrassing memories, I see now that it wasn't my fault. The wine got me. That concept—that alcohol itself is an addictive substance, and unhealthy alcohol use isn't about willpower or personal failure—was so helpful to me as I resolved to put the booze away for good.

OK, that's it, I decided. *I'm not going to drink anymore.*

And that was that.

I'm very happy that I've stopped. I tell everybody. I scream it off the rooftops that I don't want it anymore. I don't need it in my life anymore. That doesn't mean that everything about it has been easy, especially in the beginning. I've been bad-tempered and a little bitchy—my husband bore the brunt of that, but he's been so supportive and accepting through the whole process.

Not all my friends are enthusiastic, of course. When I went to a restaurant with a group of friends, one friend asked if I would be drinking. When I told him that I wouldn't be making any exceptions, he said, "What a shame."

I was in no mood for his attitude and retorted, "I'll be the one who remembers everything that we've eaten, and I'll be able to taste the food more."

He did not read the warning signal in my tone and pressed on. "Well, but you'll be drinking again one day, I'm sure."

"I'm sure I won't," I snapped.

"But—"

"What's your problem? Why is it so important to you that I drink?"

That stopped it. Perhaps I wasn't very kind, but I still think he deserved it.

In the evenings, I occasionally have little thoughts that say, *Oh, come on, you can just have one glass.*

However, as I've consistently said, *No, I'm not going to do that because tomorrow I'll be happy that I didn't,* those voices have gotten weaker and weaker. I've tried to observe the changes in my body when I'm craving wine—I get more saliva in my mouth, for example. So, when I notice that my mouth is watering, I'll very consciously go and do something else. After about six months, the cravings went away almost entirely.

These days, life is much more *real* for me. I feel more like myself. I procrastinate less at work and cuddle with my dog more. I enjoy my mornings. I have more confidence and trust in myself. I'm less stressed and less likely to lash out at my husband. This is a small example, but I'm a tidy person, and my husband is not. We often have discussions about domestic tasks—who will vacuum or do laundry or wash the dishes. This causes some conflict, as it does for most couples. When I was not as clear-headed, I'd just clean up his messes and nag him about it. Now, it's easier for me to express my needs, and I'm able to gently ask him to clean up his messes. Whether he does or not is his decision, but I'm able to say what I want and express my own needs in a calm way, rather than bottling it up until I snap at him. There is an endless number of small ways in which giving up alcohol has improved my life.

Now that I've seen the light, I want others to know the truth as well. I have to work hard to not try to convince everybody of my new way of living. So often, when I say I've quit drinking, people say, "Oh, I couldn't do what you are doing." I think, *Of course you could. You'd be amazed at how well it would work for you.* At the end of the day, I know I can't make anyone see. I can't change someone's life for them. However, I can change my own life and let it be an example of what's possible. I've found that it works—that giving up alcohol is contagious.

A friend of mine just stopped drinking, and his girlfriend has made a firm decision to drink less. More than anything else, that makes me happy and proud, that I've not only found freedom for myself but helped show someone else the way out. *This Naked Mind* has changed the world for so many people, and I'm thrilled to be part of that movement.

It really is better on the other side.

"Once you see the drug for what it is, the cause of your misery and cravings that gives you nothing in return, the desire for the drug dies."

—Annie Grace, *This Naked Mind*

NOT ANOTHER SELF-HELP BOOK
Bryan's Story

I think *This Naked Mind* saved my life.

I started drinking at sixteen and fell hopelessly in love with alcohol. It seemed to take away my anxiety. When I was drinking, I felt relaxed and happy. At first, I only imbibed on weekends. By college, I progressed to drinking midweek and anytime there was a party. I'm now sixty-eight and have been drinking quite heavily most days for the last twenty years. Though it sometimes troubled me, I just assumed I was the type who enjoyed drinking. Yes, I drank a lot, but it wasn't ruining my life.

Then, about twelve years ago, the depression set in, and I realized I was in trouble.

As a psychologist, I knew about the relationship between alcohol and depression. I decided to do something about the drinking and knew I needed to work on my unconscious mind. Once I decide to do something, I'm usually successful, so I was sure I could get this under control. I just needed the right plan. I paid for professional hypnotherapy and bought some online courses aimed at reducing alcohol intake. To my surprise, it didn't work.

I gave up and branded myself as *alcohol-dependent*. There was a sense of hopelessness about it—I expected that the drinking would kill me, sooner rather than later. While I considered AA, I felt their approach wasn't right for me.

There seemed to be nothing I could do.

Then I went on vacation across the world. Facing the prospect of an eleven-hour flight, I decided I didn't want to sit through three onboard movies and thought I'd listen to an audiobook instead. I signed up for Audible, and the first recommended book was *This Naked Mind*—probably because I'd been looking for help online.

Not another self-help book, I thought, but something drew me back, and I decided to give it a try. Perhaps it was the vacation itself. I always drink more when I'm on vacation, and I'd been worried about going into liver failure abroad.

I settled down with my first Jack Daniels and started listening. I liked the style. It was real science, not psychobabble, and I found myself enjoying the book. At dinner, I had my usual wine, and my wife asked me if I wanted cognac with my coffee. I hesitated but agreed—and that brandy at forty thousand feet was the last drink of my life.

Though Annie Grace suggests listening to two chapters at a time, I was hooked and binged through the whole thing. I'm not sure exactly when, as I listened to most of the book on that flight, but I became aware of a major shift in my thinking. If someone had suggested spontaneous sobriety to me before I started, I would have thought they were nuts—but that's what happened to me.

Before, when I arrived at a hotel, I always poured a stiff drink, but this time, I didn't want it. The whole trip, I had no desire for alcohol. Part of the vacation consisted of an all-inclusive cruise, and we had a day at sea. I decided to use that day to listen to parts of the book again, and this reinforced my newfound way of thinking. All around me, people were drinking, and I realized how normalized this had become in our society.

While we were still abroad, my GPS stopped working, and I got lost in a strange city in the dark, driving in rush hour on the side of the road opposite to home. I was stressed. I navigated using landmarks and eventually got back to my hotel. In the past, I would have reached for the bottle to reward myself for getting through it and to decompress. This time, I felt calm and did not want a drink.

I enjoy my garden, and I used to like to sit out in the evening with a glass of wine. After about three glasses, everything used to look better, and I enjoyed the experience more. Now, when I sit out, it's as if I've *had* the three glasses, even though I haven't had a drink. I needed the wine just to feel normal! How could I, a psychologist, not have seen this before?

I now know where I went wrong when I tried to quit before. All my efforts revolved around moderation rather than giving it up altogether, and for me, that was never going to work. I could not conceive of the possibility of quitting for good, and so I made myself promises that I'd only drink on vacation or while out with friends. At best, I lasted a week before I "rewarded" myself with a binge and then returned to my usual patterns. After all, how could I enjoy a night out without drinking? *This Naked Mind* showed me I could. I know some people can cut back and drink in moderation, but I am not one of them. I'm healthier and happier than I've ever been, and I'm so very grateful for Annie Grace and this wonderful book.

"You can do this, and each day will get easier. You are fighting for your life, and victory is yours."
—Annie Grace, *This Naked Mind*

A THOUSAND QUESTIONS
Lorna's Story

I didn't set out to become alcohol-free, but that's what happened. If you'd told me in the years and months before I stopped drinking about all the ways my life would change, I wouldn't have believed you. But here we are.

Like so many people in their sixties, my final decision to quit wasn't dramatic. A lot of little things over a long time led up to that moment.

It had really started when I began to notice how fast I drank and how I was counting the minutes until my husband "finally" got up from his chair to pour me wine. After all, it wasn't ladylike to haul my ass out of the chair to get my own—though I'd do that if he wasn't fast enough. Waiting for my husband to pour gave me an excuse, made me feel like I wasn't in the driver's seat. In order to be polite, I needed to drink what was put in front of me, right? One glass of wine in the evening became six, on a regular basis. A single bottle shared between us became two. I knew it wasn't good for me. Physically, I felt awful. So awful, in fact, that I started getting scared.

I'd wake up at three thirty in the morning, my mind circling on a thousand different questions: What the hell am I doing? How did that "one glass" end up being six again? Have I crossed "that line"?

Am I actually an alcoholic? Am I doomed to die early or spend the last years of my life in smoke-filled rooms, baring my soul to others who "just can't handle their booze"?

Around this time, my doctor retired, and I had to find a new one. This was an opportunity, and I started asking more questions, being more transparent about what I was worried about. I'd been experiencing weird sensations in my heart and was waking up in the middle of the night with strange feelings that made me wonder if I was on the verge of having a stroke. We ran some tests. I also decided to look into my alcohol use.

In the course of my internet research, I came across *This Naked Mind* and signed up for one of the video programs associated with the book. I was amazed at what I was learning, that there was a solution to this issue, that I was not an alcoholic—which, having grown up with a father in AA, I hadn't thought I was—but that alcohol is really ethanol: a poison taking over my mind and, ultimately, my life.

That resonated with me. It was a crazy time of exploration, and for the first time since I was pregnant with my daughter almost forty years ago, I remained alcohol-free for forty-three days. But it wasn't a permanent decision, and over time, while endeavoring to "monitor" my alcohol consumption, I fell back into old patterns. It was not only "falling" into old habits that woke me up again to what I was doing to myself, it was the horrific embarrassment of standing up from the dinner table, surrounded by family during a vacation in Mexico, taking three steps and falling face-first onto the cement floor. The look of terror on my family's faces, drunk as I was, will never leave me.

Clearly, I hadn't moderated well enough. I got home from the vacation and dug back into *This Naked Mind*. The bruise on my upper arm was a real motivator.

Over the next few months, I reread the book and really cut down on my alcohol consumption.

One evening, for no particular reason and after no particular event, I washed my wine glass and put it away. I was going to experiment with thirty days of being alcohol-free and really dig into the science. I needed to truly understand the nature of alcohol.

Well, thirty days came and went. As Annie Grace says, "You can't unlearn this stuff." Finally, it all started to sink in. In *any* quantity, alcohol is ethanol—poison. We dress it up to make it look fancy and call it cabernet sauvignon, but our body knows differently and spends all day and all night trying to get rid of the stuff. At the end of my experiment, I understood. I wanted to live hangover-free. Mostly . . . I just wanted to live.

Since then, I've gained a new coaching accreditation, passing the exam after endless hours of studying that would have made a university student cry. I've celebrated birthdays, attended weddings, gone on vacation, and had many dinners out with friends. We celebrated the birth of a new granddaughter and dealt with the bad news of my mom's cancer diagnosis and subsequent death.

That's a lot, and I did it all without a wine glass in my hand.

I'd be lying if I said there weren't times when it was hard. Damn hard.

But here's what I've learned: the "twitch" of wanting to drink went away. I didn't lose any friends. I simply *feel* better. My sleep has improved, which has been an antidote to all the stress. My mind is sharper and retains more information, from exam questions to last night's movie or yesterday's conversation. My incessant "monkey mind" has taken a back seat as I've become more present, proactive, and engaged. Our bank account isn't taking a weekly wine hit, so there's money to buy new clothes . . . a size smaller.

Mostly, I'm not catastrophizing about my own mortality, worrying about that imminent brain aneurysm, cancer diagnosis, or heart attack. That alone feels like freedom. It's not that these things can't happen, but they no longer take up space in my head in the middle of the night. I no longer worry that my drinking will trigger them.

I never was an alcoholic. Most people aren't. I hadn't crossed the "line," but I could certainly see it in the distance. If you're looking for answers about alcohol, you can probably see that line too. Or maybe you're just starting to realize that alcohol is poison, and that you don't want to poison yourself anymore. Trust me—you're right about that. I've been there.

Everyone's journey is different. The details of each person's story will vary. But I'm sure of two things as you embark on your own alcohol-free life:

You'll feel better.

And you're worth it.

> "*The key for me was changing my perspective from 'I don't get to drink' to 'I could, but I don't want to.'*"
>
> —Annie Grace, *The Alcohol Experiment*

MY LAST HANGOVER
Lisa M.'s Story

My drinking career spanned twenty-eight years. During most of that time, alcohol played a huge role in my life. After arriving home from work, I'd have a double vodka and club soda to take the edge off a rough day—and then one drink would turn into three or four. On the weekends, I could easily drink at least six cocktails. And special occasions? I always anticipated drinking at those.

"Let's go to the beach—make sure to pack the cooler!" I'd say one day. The next week, I'd realize we were going to my in-laws' house and remind my husband to not forget the vodka, whiskey, and mixers. No matter the outing, I made it a priority to ensure my need for alcohol would be fulfilled.

A few times, my husband and I tried to moderate our drinking. We said, "Let's limit ourselves to just the weekends." That usually lasted a week before one of us had a bad Thursday. And since Thursday is *almost* the weekend, it was easy to justify drinks. Then we slipped to Wednesday. Before we knew it, I was back to drinking with the same frequency as before—two to four drinks a night, almost every night. At that level, I needed to drink just to go to sleep.

The morning after my father-in-law's birthday, I woke up feeling terrible. I was exhausted, hungover . . . and I'd driven home the night before. I should have taken an Uber—I'd been too buzzed and too tired to be behind the wheel. Instead, I made a poor decision that could have had disastrous consequences. I lay there forced to confront a terrifying question: Did I have a problem with drinking?

I'm fortunate to have a loving husband, and I opened up to him about my concerns. He paused and then suggested neither of us drink for thirty days. My eyes got big. Going thirty days alcohol-free was a scary thought. But I took a deep breath and said, "OK. Let's give it a shot."

We signed up for a thirty-day no-alcohol challenge. I also joined a Facebook group affiliated with the challenge. In addition to posting in that Facebook group, I kept a written journal, where I listed my "why": Why had I enlisted in the challenge? What would I gain from not drinking for thirty days?

Throughout that month, I paid close attention to how I was feeling. Two weeks into the challenge, I started to feel more energetic. I also realized that this was the first time in as long as I could remember that I'd gone two weeks without alcohol. We went to a concert at an amphitheater and enjoyed ourselves with refreshing club sodas with lime—which is now my favorite drink! We left the concert and went out for flavored coffee and dark chocolate. A week later, we went to a wedding and had a blast—no alcohol needed. We hung out with family, and while they drank their alcohol, my husband and I enjoyed our flavored sparkling water.

Throughout these thirty days, my morning runs got easier. I wasn't hitting the snooze button, because I woke up before the alarm. I even lost sixteen pounds. And I found myself questioning whether or not I even wanted to drink anymore.

Two days after the challenge officially ended, we hung out with some friends who enjoy drinking. Though I was still wrestling through a lot of questions about what I wanted my relationship with alcohol to look like, I decided to split a bottle of champagne with my husband and a friend. We left that restaurant and headed to a sports bar where I ordered a vodka and club soda. I took a sip of the vodka soda and instantly had a headache.

No, I thought. This wasn't what I wanted. I pushed the glass away.

The next weekend, we went to DC because my husband had a professional music audition. At the hotel, I had a craving for champagne. I figured I'd just have a glass—no big deal. Well, I had a glass of champagne, and then a glass of wine, and then another glass of champagne at dinner.

I woke up the next morning feeling good. It gave me a false sense of security, lulling me into thinking that I was doing fine. So, that evening, I started with a glass of champagne, followed by a bottle of champagne, and then two more glasses. We walked back to our hotel and somehow got to the room safely.

I say *somehow* because I don't remember it. I woke up at five the next morning, feeling like I'd been hit by a bus. I didn't remember the last hour of the night. And I knew I never wanted to do that again.

My husband dumped the leftover alcohol. I managed a couple more hours of sleep before we checked out of the hotel. And when we got on the plane, I decided to finish reading *This Naked Mind*, which I'd downloaded a week or two earlier. As I read, I kept asking myself, *What do I do now?*

The truth is that I was scared out of my mind, but deep down, I knew that letting go of alcohol was the best thing I could do for myself. I set the book down and started scrolling through some photos from the trip. Then I stumbled on a post I'd screenshotted. It said: *The goal isn't to be sober. The goal is to love yourself so much that you don't need a drink.*

And in that moment, I was done. That morning's hangover had been my last.

Here I am now, alcohol-free and loving it. I have not felt this good in so long. I'm crying as I write this, because I'm so proud of this life I'm creating. For the first time in a long time, I'm proud of me.

I go to bars, games, and parties with friends, and I enjoy it all without a single drop of alcohol. After the first football game I attended without drinking, I didn't have to worry how we were going to get home two hours from the stadium. We could just drive—sober and free. I can't begin to describe the sense of satisfaction I had. That memory alone brings tears to my eyes.

Alcohol—consciously and unconsciously—holds no place in my life because I see it for what it is: poison. I'm so grateful for my new beginning and so excited to see what the future holds.

"Take a stand for yourself, realizing you want nothing to do with the groupthink of alcohol. Be brave and be different."
—Annie Grace, *This Naked Mind*

I JUST DON'T WANT TO
Andrew's Story

Hey, I'm Andrew, and I choose not to drink.

I could drink if I wanted to. I just don't want to.

I went out for lunch a couple of weeks ago with some friends. One guy was falling asleep at the table. He'd been drinking since the morning. That's not the sort of person I really want to be. I'm not going to judge him—that's his world. His experiences have been different from mine. But I feel so good that I'm in the moment, and in four hours' time, I'll still be in the moment, and tomorrow I won't have suffered from making myself cloudy through a deluge of alcohol. I won't have the hangover. I won't have any of that.

The friend apologized to me the next day, and I assured him that it was OK. And it really was, because I've been in his shoes. There were times during my drinking career when I turned into a person I didn't particularly like. I always described myself as a happy drunk, but sometimes I really wasn't very nice. Maybe it's a character flaw, but I think your filters fall away when you drink, and you don't have the nails to think, *Hey, I shouldn't say that*. Your bullshit filter stops working, and you just let it out.

My first drink was probably when I was about age three. My family had these souvenir sherry bottles from the Barossa Valley, and I quite liked the flavor. From what my sister has told me, I was probably a little bit intoxicated as a toddler, just because I liked the taste.

As I got into my early teens, I ended up experimenting with alcohol, mostly beer and the odd spirit, but it wasn't until I got older that my alcohol use took off.

I joined a job with a fairly strong drinking culture and lots of camaraderie. I took to that like a duck to water. It seemed like a way of socializing, letting off steam, and putting problems in the bag so I didn't have to look at them. By the time I got to about age forty, maybe a little earlier, I realized I was drinking too much, and so I started the cycle: I'd give it up for a month, three months, six months.

I got to the point where I was drinking six, eight, ten, twelve beers in a session. I'd look at the bottles in the morning and think, *Shit, here's someone who's got a problem.*

But other people would say, "At least you're not drinking Scotch." I think I used those sorts of things to excuse it.

Anyway, I ended up going to a psychiatrist and was diagnosed with depression, anxiety, and post-traumatic stress. But the biggest deal was admitting to myself and saying out loud, "Hey, I'm probably an alcoholic too."

I went to AA, and they do great things, but it wasn't for me. I think I gave alcohol up for six months that time, but then I busted and started back with half-strength beer. Lo and behold! My brain really did say, "Wow, you're back. Feed me, feed me, feed me." I fed it, and I fed it plenty.

My lady ended up telling me that we'd implode if I kept drinking. And we almost did. But she gave me a copy of *This Naked Mind*, and I read it feverishly. What really worked for me was that the book didn't tell me not to drink. It didn't tell me things I didn't know. It just said them in a different way that made far more sense to me.

So I'm choosing not to drink now, not denying myself. And look, I drink zero-alcohol beer, because I actually like the taste of beer. I even still have some leftover bottles of gin in my cupboard, and I haven't touched them. I don't have a craving for alcohol, and I don't want it. Life's better without it.

And it's freeing to know that I don't have to put all these labels or rules on myself. If I ever choose to have a drink on vacation—not that I'm planning to—I don't have to beat myself up for it. I'm not a rule-follower, and any lecture that sounds like an angry parent makes me want to do the opposite.

I don't want to be "Hey, I'm Andrew, and I'm an alcoholic." So, I'm not.

Instead, I say, "Hey, I'm Andrew, and I choose not to drink." I choose to feel good. I choose to be clear-headed. I choose not to suffer.

I choose not to drink.

"*Making one big decision with all your mind, body, and spirit liberates you from the hundreds of daily decisions around alcohol that sap your energy.*"

—Annie Grace, *The Alcohol Experiment*

THIS NAKED MIND AND TEA
Stephanie's Story

I read the first half of *This Naked Mind* at night—drunk. I read the second half at night too—this time sober. I'd ordered it from the library after someone recommended it on a keto Facebook page. At first, I buried it in a pile of other books because I was too embarrassed to look at it. *I should be able to overcome this drinking thing on my own, shouldn't I?* My drinking was out of control, but I'd overcome so many other things.

I'd had a horrible childhood, but for a long time, I pretended everything was fine. I did the extra credit, got good grades, played sports. I was even in band.

At age sixteen, I was sexually assaulted. That changed everything. I lost my trust in people and began drinking and smoking weed to cope, to numb out. By seventeen, I was a mom of twins. The babies were born prematurely and had many health problems. To make matters worse, I still lived with my parents, who resented me—though they did help out with the kids.

I was still trying to make good grades and look like I had my life together while being there for my kids. But my parents' verbal abuse grew worse, and I began to rely more heavily on alcohol and drugs to get through each day. After a whirlwind romance, I married a drug addict when I was nineteen. That only made my situation harder. (Shocking, right?)

Life was so, so difficult. I was trying to be a responsible adult and keep it all together—working, taking my kids to physical therapy, picking out a wheelchair for my son. My then-husband, meanwhile, just drank, smoked weed, fished, and cheated on me. Throughout that marriage, I kept drinking. How else could I cope?

After seven years, I finally worked up the courage to leave him—only to find out I was pregnant. I ended up staying with him for a while longer. But one day he told me he didn't love me—never had, never would—and that he was leaving me for another woman.

I felt relieved. Life was going to get better. I even realized that I didn't have to drink anymore—that I could garden or read books now that I was rid of that relationship. But, of course, the drinking crept back into my life again—this time as wine. Wine and whiskey are socially acceptable, right?

Over time, my life grew more stable. But it seemed like unhappiness was following me everywhere I went. I couldn't understand it. *Why* was I so unhappy? I had a great career as a photographer. I got married again, and my husband loved me unconditionally. But I was carrying around so much psychological baggage.

I was diagnosed with PTSD and depression after someone—actually, the woman my now-jailed ex-husband left me for—recommended a great therapist in town. In treatment—brainspotting, specifically—I uncovered so many past emotions and traumas I'd stuffed away. And something amazing happened. I began to heal. My marriage began to heal.

But I was still drinking too much.

I woke up hungover every day. When I took the dogs on their morning walk, I didn't want to run into anyone because I felt like shit. And it wasn't like the alcohol was helping me have a good time with people. I shut down and stopped talking when I was drinking so that I wouldn't sound like an a-hole. Alcohol was doing nothing positive for me, and I knew it. And that embarrassed me. I could look at all I'd overcome and see how much progress I was making. Why couldn't I get over this alcohol thing?

I'm so grateful that someone recommended *This Naked Mind*. The book made so much sense to me—despite having read the first half of it drunk! I mulled it over for a few days . . . and then we ran out of soda water. I'm a vodka soda girl, so I needed to go to the store. But I decided not to. Instead, I made some tea. I wanted that instead.

And I haven't had a drink since. *This Naked Mind* and tea have been my saving grace—I can drink as much tea as I want and still feel great! These days I'm also listening through the *This Naked Mind* podcast and experiencing profound gratitude. I'm so thankful for my life and for the freedom that not drinking has given me. I know there's a long path ahead, but I'm so optimistic about my future.

After all—I've overcome so many other things. I know I can do this too.

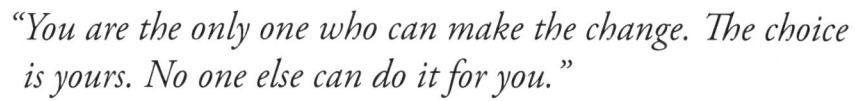

"You are the only one who can make the change. The choice is yours. No one else can do it for you."

—Annie Grace, *The Alcohol Experiment*

I HAVE A CHOICE
Robbie's Story

I parallel park on a raw, rainy April afternoon. I'm late. Again. I'm exhausted and can barely make it to any place I'm supposed to be.

Through the wet glass, I watch the smokers huddle across the street before their AA meeting. Are they as miserable as they look? As miserable as I feel? Or do I just assume they're miserable, because they once drank too much? Because they're trying to not drink now? That's the choice, right? Drink more than I want to, or spend the rest of my life trying not to.

I don't want to go to daily meetings. And I'm not looking for a higher power. This may be just the way it goes for me. High-functioning, capable wife, mother, daughter, sister, friend, nurse. I wake each morning, feeling like crap but with fresh resolve. Then that evening arrives, like a wheel in a rut, and the wine glass is full before I've had a chance to put up a fight.

I earned it. I like it. I want it.

I don't think about the headache and the fitful sleep that awaits me. Or the next day lost to fatigue and anxiety and toxic self-talk. This glass belongs in my hand. My lips belong on this glass. At this moment, tomorrow doesn't exist.

I worked for a newspaper for many years. I'm a proud news

junkie. I want—no, I *need*—to know what's going on. But these days, the news makes me sad and angry and frustrated and scared. I drink, and drink more, to blunt the rising distress.

In the dark fuzz of another sleepless night, I check the tweets of one of my favorite sources. A lawyer-turned-activist who tells it like it is, usually with a ray of hope inserted somewhere, somehow. There on her feed is a big pour of red, backlit and glittering. She says she's beginning a popular experiment the next day. An attempt at no drinking for thirty days. An experiment? That word is like a tiny anchor that drops and settles in my mind. I can do an experiment.

A few days later, I search for The Alcohol Experiment. I sign up. That's a Saturday. The next day is Easter and dinner out with family. Wine is a must. But I set it as my start day anyway. Feels like I'm setting myself up to fail on day one. But maybe what I need is this decision imposed on me. A plan and accountability offer a sliver of hope.

Hope. It's why each morning starts out somewhat fresh. It's why I sat and watched the AA group from my car. It's why I stored The Alcohol Experiment in my foggy brain when I heard about it. It's why I had visions of my future self that looked so different from the person I was then. Sleeping soundly. Rising with ideas. Following through. Loving unconditionally. Nuzzling a grandchild.

Day one with family. I don't want to stand out without a drink. But I'm also not one to hold back. Before I can be asked, my words stumble out: "I'm doing a thirty-day experiment." I discover it's a much bigger deal to me, so I sink into oblivion, with the tumult of my brain to keep me company. Like a six-year-old, it keeps grabbing at my sleeve, pleading with me, telling me I'm mean. I do my best to ignore it, stand firm.

Day one is a success, if you can call it that. My head is tired.

The next week brings a subtle wonder, at least in the mornings. I did it, again? Wow. Can this continue? For thirty days? Then I can drink again, but with the power of thirty days behind me, to learn to drink the right way. Wouldn't that be something? I'll prove I can go thirty days. That magical number. Surely that will nip my misery in the bud, and drinking will be fun again.

Week two begins, I feel strong. A whole week! I'm stronger than I thought. No, wait. I knew I was strong. But not this kind of strong. And I feel better. My head. My gut. My energy. My confidence. It'll be so great to drink alongside this new, controlled me.

The next week is tough. Not because I want to break the streak. But because I feel too good. It can't be just the absence of alcohol that has me sleeping and tackling the day better than I have in . . . ever? I feel brand new.

I clean out the attic. We've lived in this house for twenty-eight years. My husband's grandmother's relics are in all the far corners. I've been wanting to do this since moving in.

Could life be good, long-term, without alcohol? Nah . . . maybe?

It's the final week; I'm scared. I don't want the Experiment to end. I know I can go thirty days. I'm almost there. But I want to keep the leash on. I don't want to make my own decisions about drinking. The Experiment is safe and warm and kind. I am not safe and warm and kind when I drink. But maybe I can be now, having cultivated the non-drinking me.

Day thirty-one. I have a choice. But I don't want it.

Tell me what to do.

Fear is not a healthy motivator, but it's in this state that I spend the next few weeks. My fear of drinking is greater than my fear of not. Uncomfortable, but effective. And the more days I accumulate, the better I feel. Like an advent calendar of sober surprises. Sleep. Energy. Calm. Love. Humor. Clear skin. An abundance of compassion. Relaxed waistbands.

Thoughts squirm into my head. *I think I might be done. Moderation feels like a lot of work. This doesn't suck. I like this me. A lot.*

I respect science. The thirty days included solid science. Facts about alcohol I could never unlearn. Alcohol is the third-leading preventable cause of death in the United States. Alcohol is a depressive and a stimulant. The depressive effects are immediate. The stimulation comes later, when you're trying to sleep. It's your body's tireless quest to achieve that elusive state of homeostasis that alcohol prevents. Our resources go into processing and eliminating alcohol from our bodies, forcing other bodily functions to take a backseat to this emergency. A constant state of emergency. In our bodies. And in our minds. Anxiety thrives in a state of crisis.

We reach for a drink to hush the anxiety. The cycle begins anew.

So what do I do with all this unforgettable information? I understand the substance, the chemistry of it in our bodies. The eye-popping statistics. So why does everyone still do it? Still drink? Because it's the most pushed and unquestioned societal rite of passage there is. The cool kids do it. The fun and balanced adults do it. You only die from it if you're unlucky, or God forbid, you can't control a highly addictive substance. The bottle's in your court. Figure it out. Or suffer in silence.

Outrageous.

And that's why my week four was so frightening. I knew drinking was bad for me. I knew I'd been sold a big, fat lemon. But I had beliefs about my own relationship with alcohol that felt unmovable. I wrote two lists about alcohol on day one of the Experiment. I wrote both of these statements: I control it. I don't like feeling powerless.

What?

How could both be true?

I didn't control it. It controlled me. No wonder I felt powerless.

So, I knew I was strong. I knew I was a survivor. I knew I wanted to live. I needed to question every belief about alcohol I took as truth. I needed to learn how to experience life without wine. Which meant *actually* experiencing it. The real highs and real lows, and everything in between.

I began with this thought: I'm not sure I can stop drinking. And that made me feel confused, anxious, and so very stuck. It made me irritable. And it encouraged me to drink more. Those feelings are not fun, and I'd practiced squashing them for a long time.

What a messy, messy loop. But could I find an antidote to that frightening thought? I could. And it was this: *What if I can?*

And that's how my experiment went on. And how my life began anew.

For a time, early on, I still salivated when I found a wine list in front of me. Pavlov's dog. I wondered if the clerks in my favorite package stores thought about me. But now there's no tug of the steering wheel to turn in. No bottle for home. It doesn't enter my mind, which I find amazing every time I take stock.

That tiny anchor I put down many months ago is now firmly entrenched. It began to dig in as I accumulated lots of firsts under my belt, and then it solidified as I repeated those events alcohol-free, over and over. Dinners out. Celebrations. Events. Time with close friends. Tough days and challenging emotions. Nights home alone.

I came to trust, and then believe, that I can have a good time anywhere. That my alcohol-free laughter and tears are the real thing. I can weather the not-so-great days with perspective and resources. Best of all, my anxiety about the unknown has morphed into curiosity and action.

And from this place, I care for myself, every day. I'm still a news junkie, but I can take it in, heartbreaking as much of it is, and take action toward making the world a better place. It begins with me.

Well actually, it began with The Alcohol Experiment! I'm sure of that and am forever grateful. That's why I became a This Naked Mind coach. Learning to live free of alcohol is one of the greatest gifts I've received. What better way to help heal a world in pain and in need of hope than to pay that forward? There's so much good just waiting to be tapped.

"Really, you are amazing. And you owe it to yourself to put some thought and intention into how you want to go forward from here. How do you want your life to go?"

—Annie Grace, *The Alcohol Experiment*

QUITTING COLD TURKEY
Mike S.'s Story

As I see it, people need two things when they're looking to drink: time and money. I got drunk a handful of times in high school and partied my first couple years of college, but I didn't have the time or money to get too sucked into it. And all the partying came to a halt when I started dating the woman who would become my wife.

You see, when you're newly in love and maintaining your other friendships and trying to pass your college classes, there just isn't enough time and money for alcohol to be all that involved. I worked for a year after graduation while my girlfriend took a fifth year of advanced education training. And then we got married the following year. As recently graduated newlyweds, our idea of a big romantic night out was a couple of Subway sandwiches and a six-pack for the two of us. Even though I grappled with a lot of anxiety, I didn't turn to alcohol to cope—we just didn't have the money.

Once our sons were born, we threw ourselves into parenting. Our time went toward our boys, and our money went toward diapers and formula and the mortgage. I was very much a moderate drinker—a couple beers on the weekend, a party here and there, one or two weddings where we got really smashed. But that was the exception. My focus was elsewhere—with my wife and my sons.

And then, one by one, the dice were thrown, and things began to change. Six years ago, when my kids were about eleven and thirteen, we went on a family vacation to an all-inclusive resort in Jamaica. The boys met a bunch of kids their own age, and the parents all sat around drinking beach cocktails and eating jerk chicken. It was on this trip that I developed a taste for rum. It was one of those vacations where everything had rum in it. You woke up in the morning, and they offered you a coffee, asking, "Would you like some rum in that?"

"Oh sure," I responded every time.

And so, when we came back from that trip, I bought a bottle here and a bottle there and stashed them away to drink every now and then. And "every now and then" became a little more frequently. It built up over the next year or so, until it got to a level where I started hiding things around the house. And that was the first warning bell that something was off. But you can always come up with an excuse to drink—you can drink to celebrate, to commiserate, to avoid stress. So this slow build-up continued for a couple years. If I'm being honest, I was covering up my anxieties and insecurities with alcohol. But I didn't realize it at the time.

In 2015, my mom was diagnosed with lung cancer. That came as a shock to my system. You see, my parents had been big drinkers and smokers when I was young, but my mom had quit cold turkey twenty years previously. She'd just woken up one day and decided she was done. And she never took another sip of alcohol or smoked another cigarette.

But it still got her in the end.

My mom's last months were a time of profound stress. There were so many layers of grief, and underneath all that, there was guilt—I was the oldest, but I wasn't always present because I had my family, we lived an hour away, and I commuted an hour in the other direction to work every day. I wasn't available to help out when she was ill and going through treatment. She relied on my younger brother and sister.

Then, around the same time that she passed away, I found out my dad was having health problems too. Heart disease was taking a toll on his body, and he needed surgery. He pulled through, but again, I had to cope with the guilt of not being as available for him as I wanted to be. And I drank that pain away.

But you wouldn't have known it. I was still high functioning at work. I was hiding the extra bottles—I had a whole system. I thought I had everything under control. And then my company downsized, and I was let go—right before Christmas—from a job I'd loved for eleven years. It sideswiped me. I wasn't expecting it at all. But it came with a nice severance package, so I decided to pull myself together and look for a job after the holidays. We'd already pre-booked a trip to Cuba over New Year's, so we decided to go on the trip and enjoy the vacation before I got too focused on the job market.

It was another all-inclusive resort. You can imagine how much I drank on that trip.

When I got home, the job hunt began. My previous company extended us some transitional services, so I threw myself into learning how to be on the job market again. And I was all over that. I loved it—it got me up in the morning. I'd sit in front of my computer and say, "OK, what are we going to do today?" I maintained that exuberance for probably three or four months. But when unemployment began to drag on, old insecurities started cropping up: "I'm not good enough. Why aren't I getting a job? Why aren't things happening for me?"

Summer rolled in, and I still didn't have a job. So, rather than doing the applications at the kitchen table, I took them out on the back deck and sat there all afternoon with a drink in my hand.

After all, if I looked hard enough, I could always find a reason to drink.

Around that time, I had my annual physical. Some of my liver enzyme numbers were elevated.

The doctor asked, "How many drinks do you have? What do you drink a week?"

And, of course, I lied and took the numbers down a little bit. But then I told him, "Probably more than I should be."

"OK," he said, "you need to moderate."

Then I asked him for a referral to a therapist for the anxiety I was feeling about the job hunt. I left the appointment with my heart pounding and a cold determination in my chest. That day marked the first time I really dove into alcohol reduction. After what had happened to my mom, I felt an overwhelming need to bring my numbers back into the normal ranges.

I went to a few sessions of therapy, and the therapist flagged me quickly when I talked about my history. "You realize this isn't just normal drinking you're describing here?" She put me on a schedule, and said, "OK, what I want you to do is moderate. Write down exactly what you drink every week."

And when I went back for the next session, I told her, "OK, I had two beers this night, one beer that night." Whatever it was. With my mom's death fresh in my mind and the fear that I'd damaged my liver permanently, that actually worked quite well for about five or six weeks.

But my control started to slip a little. I'd postpone writing down what I'd had to drink, or I'd intentionally "forget" about a drink so I didn't have to tell the therapist about it. Eventually, I got a new job and stopped going to therapy. When my next round of bloodwork came back, looking good, I picked up my habits all over again. Drinks with coworkers. Nights out with friends. A trip to Vegas.

I was drinking a lot, running through my usual justifications. But this time, I knew something was wrong. It started when I was getting ready for a social event with a group of friends—a dinner we'd already bought tickets for. But the cold-sweat fear hit me all at once. "I'm not going," I told my wife. "I can't do it. I just can't go."

She raised her eyebrows. "Why not?"

To this day, I can't answer that question. I can't explain it now, and I certainly couldn't then. I shook my head. "I just can't go."

She let it pass. But I couldn't. Because I knew this was another warning bell. I was starting to pull away from people, to withdraw from friends and activities I loved. It was a path I didn't want to go down, but I didn't know how to stop it from happening.

Two weeks later, I'd had a few drinks at home—a couple more than I wanted my wife to know about. But I was pretty confident in my ability to hide it, and I went upstairs to ask her a question. And she absolutely shut me down. She said, "I'm not going to talk to you because you've been drinking."

It was another warning bell. These days, she worries that she enabled my drinking, but she's always been so perceptive. If she'd tried to call me on the alcohol any earlier or given me an ultimatum, I wouldn't have been able to hear it. I think she could sense that.

I lived in this in-between space for about a week, knowing she wasn't comfortable with my drinking, knowing I wasn't comfortable with it, either, knowing something needed to change. And finally, the last warning bell rang.

She went to bed early one night, and I broke out a bottle I hadn't told her about—one I'd hidden from her. I finished it off but forgot the bottle on the kitchen counter before I went to bed. When I came downstairs the next morning, the bottle was still sitting there. She hadn't touched it. She'd left it for me to deal with. And the pain seared through me. I loved this woman as much as I had in those head-spinning college years. We'd raised two children together, built a wonderful life. And I didn't want to hurt her.

I walked into the other room, looked her in the eye, and said, "I'm done. That's it. I'm not drinking anymore."

I think my mom would have been proud of me.

The story doesn't end there, of course. I knew I needed to deal with the underlying anxiety I'd been masking with alcohol. The next Monday, I called my doctor for an appointment, and he put me on anti-anxiety medication and recommended cognitive-behavioral therapy. The therapy was amazing and gave me so many tools to take charge of my life.

I started reading books, too. One of those books was *This Naked Mind*. I read it in two days. It was almost like a playbook for my life—aligning the conscious and unconscious minds in a way that allowed me to just say, "I'm done" and mean it made so much sense. It gave language to my experience, and to what my mom had done when she quit cold turkey all those years ago.

Now I'm so grateful for this new non-drinking way of life. My wife and boys have been so supportive. It's been the best decision I've ever made. It's opened doors I hadn't even imagined it could. I have confidence to meet people—like my favorite bands at meet-and-greets or attendees at This Naked Mind Live in Denver—because I know I won't make an ass out of myself by being drunk. I've had the opportunity to put my time and money to better uses than alcohol—especially time with my family and friends. Now, I'm welcoming the path ahead rather than fearing it.

Alcohol can't deceive me anymore, and that's a beautiful thing.

"Before you drank alcohol, you didn't miss it; you didn't think about it. You were happy and free."

—Annie Grace, *This Naked Mind*

"It's freeing to know you're in control."
—Annie Grace, *The Alcohol Experiment*

NO ANESTHESIA
Gerri's Story

At age twenty, I started working in corporate America and quickly found out that the way to success and promotions back in the '80s and '90s was through drinking with the right people after work. If you didn't drink, you were, at best, interrogated about it and, at worst, ostracized. We had alcohol at home too. My husband and I would crack open a beer every afternoon as soon as we got home from picking up the kids from daycare.

In my mid-thirties, my drinking was really getting out of control. Even though I'd been a social drinker, I started bingeing alcohol—often a quart of tequila in a weekend—to deal with the stress and pain in my life.

Then my husband and I came home drunk from a football game, and my oldest son was standing in the kitchen. *Oh my gosh,* I thought, *he's going to be getting his driver's permit soon, and we're driving drunk in front of him!*

This troubled me, and one Monday morning, I woke up and thought, *I'm going to try not to drink, but I'm not going to tell anyone.*

I didn't touch a drop for fifteen years. Not a sip of champagne at a wedding, nothing. I was completely free of alcohol. It was what we call "spontaneous sobriety." Even though we still had beer in the house, I had absolutely no desire to ever feel buzzed or drunk again.

In hindsight, the problem was that I did it for my kids and not for myself. Being the best mom I could be was the single most important thing in my life. But when my kids grew up and my world crumbled, so did my sobriety.

Almost fifteen years to the day after I quit drinking, my husband of twenty-two years announced he was leaving me. He'd been having an affair with an old girlfriend and wanted to be with her.

To say I was devastated was an understatement. I lost quite literally everything—my husband, my marriage, my home, his entire family unit (who took his side), my status in the neighborhood, my friendships, my finances. Even my two sons distanced themselves from me. I had to move into an apartment I couldn't really afford, and I didn't even have access to money to hire an attorney—but my ex sure did! Suffice it to say, he hired a ruthless lawyer, and I was left with my clothes and the furniture from the house, along with a small amount of alimony. I had to file for bankruptcy.

I felt like I just wanted to die. I didn't actually try to kill myself, but I didn't care in the least about my life or health or what I was doing to my body. I started drinking all day, every day to numb the pain. I'd wake up in the morning and have a shot. I'd get through work by hiding those small bottles of wine in my purse.

Surely I'll be able to stop when I want to, I reasoned. *I did it before.* But I couldn't sustain any change this time, because I was drinking for a very different reason—to kill the pain of rejection and abandonment.

By the grace of God, I did find an amazing man, whom I married a year later. He knew of my drinking problem and said he loved the real me. But despite his steady care, I still hit rock bottom.

I ended up with a DUI, crashed my car, got my license taken away for a year, and lost access to my four beautiful grandchildren. My son and daughter-in-law refused to speak to me for over a year.

I lost everything and everyone to this downward spiral, except my new husband, but even he was struggling to deal with my horrific binge drinking and the terrible things I'd do and say while I was drunk. I felt God wouldn't even listen to my prayers or shrieks of agony over what I'd become, that he couldn't possibly love me as I was.

I knew I couldn't go on for much longer, and part of me didn't want to. I thought it was all my fault, because I couldn't stop on my own—or even in treatment at the hospital. My pain seemed indescribable to anyone else—it was physical, as if someone was ripping my heart and stomach out of my body with no anesthesia.

Except for alcohol. Alcohol was the only anesthetic that temporarily deadened the pain.

I was beginning to lose all hope. I didn't want to leave a legacy of alcohol-induced suicide, but I'd never intended to model alcohol abuse, either.

Then *This Naked Mind* saved my life. A thirty-day alcohol-free challenge from a woman named Annie Grace popped up on my Facebook feed. I was immediately interested and began my journey to become alcohol-free then and there. I went through the challenges and the books, and everything Annie said resonated with me.

Still, I had so much trauma to unpack. I couldn't seem to get completely free from the grip of alcohol. I'd go weeks—even months—without alcohol and then drink again when something I couldn't handle or control began to cause too much pain.

But I was making progress, so I signed up for one of the live events, desperate for help to get really, truly free. At the check-in table, I told one of the women that all I could think about was that I should be dead.

During the live event, I learned about This Naked Mind coaching, and I absolutely knew I had to sign up. And I had just enough money left from my inheritance from my mother to cover the cost of a year's worth of coaching. I signed up, paid, and came home from the event, telling my husband that I was so excited because I really felt that this was the answer to my prayers.

I was right. Since that day, so many things have changed.

I'd been terrified of becoming alcohol-free, because I'd worried I'd have no escape from the pain I had no tools to handle. But through that coaching program, I found people who cared about me even in my current state! They wanted to help me learn to love myself again and rid myself of the shame and guilt. They *got* me. They didn't judge me or throw me under the bus or say, "Stop drinking or else." They truly, sincerely, authentically wanted to help me because they knew how alcohol had deceived and stolen from me.

They'd been there too.

They saved my life.

With the help of this tribe of people, my newfound knowledge of the science of alcohol, and the tools Annie Grace discovered through her research for *This Naked Mind*, I was finally able to become alcohol-free.

This time, I did it for myself.

The journey wasn't always easy, but it was far easier than staying addicted to the poison that was killing me. What a beautiful life it is to be free from the chains of alcohol that had bound me up. It's an indescribable miracle to be able to really feel life—the good and the bad. What a gift from God!

always highly functional. But there came a point where I realized it was holding me back.

Alcohol came into my life when I was young. I was raised by a single mother and often stayed for long stints with other relatives when she moved from state to state. As is the case for many, my extended-family functions always seemed to revolve around alcohol. If we were celebrating, we drank. If we were sad, we drank. It didn't matter what we were doing—there was always alcohol around.

The first time I drank—I was fifteen—I snuck a beer from my older cousins, guys who were about twenty and really like father figures to me. Over time, the one beer I'd try to hide from them turned into two, which turned into three, which turned into a twelve-pack. Before I knew it, I was drinking quite a bit. I never thought it was a big deal. I was always an honor roll student.

By the time I got to college, I was small, only 155 pounds, but I could drink everyone under the table. I was the champion of every drinking game. It was crazy how much my friends and I drank, but I was still on the dean's list with a 4.0. I was functioning just fine, and it didn't seem like it was holding me back.

A few years later, I spent a lot of time closing deals with clients at a marketing firm. That meant I was going out with potential clients after work and attending a lot of networking events, many of which revolved around drinking. I found myself leaving my family to go drinking most nights, staying out long after the work event actually ended. I'd tell my wife that I made a good contact and stayed late. Sometimes it was true, and sometimes it wasn't—so drinking led to a lot of lying to my family and spending a lot of time away from them. As the stress at work grew, so did my drinking. I took on partial ownership of the company, and the other co-owner and I would drink when we had something to celebrate or when we had something to stress over. In the entrepreneur life, there's always something to stress over.

Pretty soon, we were hitting the bar every day, often leaving work early so that we'd have more time to drink. We'd find ourselves still drinking after we were supposed to have gone home. I'd call my wife to say I had an emergency meeting and needed to stay late. She knew I was full of it, but I still kept on doing it.

At the same time, the company was experiencing success, and I was keeping up with my self-improvement practices—even if it meant I was getting up to meditate on three or four hours of sleep. Just like in high school and college, I was doing well. So, I kept telling myself that everything was OK.

But in truth, it was putting a huge strain on my marriage. Day after day, I was letting my wife down. Not to mention all the time I was wasting at the bar instead of spending with my kids. At work, there was a lot of untapped potential we didn't take advantage of because we were rushing out early to drink.

The bottom line was that I was stagnating. And worse—I knew it. Despite all my successes, I'd hit a plateau. I couldn't continue to expand the way I wanted to while living the way I was living. I knew the man I needed to be wasn't in alignment with the man I was.

At a conference, I was challenged to identify my "big domino": the one habit that, if changed, could literally change everything. I knew exactly what that domino was—if I could improve my relationship with alcohol, I could get rid of a heavy weight that was holding me down in almost every area of my life. When I thought about the one thing that could improve my health, strengthen my relationship with my family, deepen my spirituality, and give me the edge I needed to grow my business, it was crystal-clear that I needed to cut back on my drinking. I wrote it in the event journals . . . and then went back home and promptly showed up on my usual stool at the bar. I repeated this over and over again for years, knowing what I needed to do but not taking action on it.

One morning, I woke up feeling really crappy. I'd stayed up drinking until two or three o'clock, and when my alarm rang at six thirty in the morning, I didn't feel like going to work. *The only way to fix this is to have a drink,* I thought. *You can't be hungover if you don't stop drinking.*

So, I dropped my kids off at school and went to a bar that opened early for a couple shots. In absolute misery, I took those two shots, realizing that this wasn't right. This was absolutely not in alignment with the person I wanted to be, and I needed to do something different. It was time to make a change.

I started reading *This Naked Mind*, in part because I was hoping it would help me moderate instead of quitting. I especially liked that the book said I could keep drinking as I read. *This is awesome,* I thought. *It's really going to teach me how to moderate.*

Then, as I read the book, of course, I started to realize the huge impact alcohol was having on my life and decided moderation wasn't for me, that it was time to quit. The book helped me see alcohol for what it was and that life, advertising, and the media had ingrained in me the idea that I needed to drink to deal with emotions—and that idea had all been a lie.

So I quit. And I don't want to say that everything in my life is better as a result, but the truth is that I'm hard-pressed to find a single area of my life that wasn't improved by that choice. I'm not lying to my wife or drinking and driving. I'm going to bed at a reasonable time. I'm spending more time with my family. My wife and I have weekly date nights and rarely fight anymore. Our relationship feels like it did when we first started dating. I have daddy/daughter date nights with my girls, and I tuck my son into bed every night. I meditate every day for at least thirty minutes. My health has improved—I've lost forty pounds. Professionally, we added a new seven-figure division to our business and are working on a second that looks like it's going to be even bigger. And all that success at work feels effortless because it's the result of me being there and fully present. I cannot overstate what this has done for me. It really was the "big domino" that helped everything fall into place.

Above all, I go to bed every day a better person than I was when I woke up that morning. And that's something I have a chance to be grateful for every day.

"When you build on a foundation of success, the next step becomes achievable. You don't expect to run a marathon without first running a mile."

—Annie Grace, *The Alcohol Experiment*

IT ENDS HERE
Kari's Story

"Thank you" will never be enough.

This Naked Mind opened my eyes to an alcohol-free life that's both fulfilling and genuinely more fun than I could have imagined. A little over a year ago, I read a blog about mommy wine culture that stabbed me through the heart. My nightly wine was a bad habit—I knew that. But somehow I simultaneously didn't realize how common it was or that there was another way to live.

That blog post introduced me to Annie Grace's Alcohol Experiment. I decided to at least give it a try.

I drank heavily from late high school all the way into my thirties. In hindsight, I'm stunned at my early drinking years. In my teens and early twenties, I regularly blacked out. At the time, it didn't seem like a problem. It was just how everyone had their fun. My drinking got a little tamer over time. I went from drinking some during the week and bingeing on weekends to a daily, moderate intake in my late twenties onward. Law school gets the credit for that. At twenty-eight, I decided to go back to school and enrolled in an evening law program. I worked a full-time job during the day and went to class three or four nights a week. To be successful in school, I had no choice but to slow down my drinking.

After graduation, I worked at a small firm, and I had two children in a three-year span. True to form, I began pouring wine the second I walked in the door in the evening. For several years, I drank three to four glasses a night during the week and a little more on the weekends. Because I wasn't bingeing, I felt what I was doing was an appropriate way to unwind after a long day. I deserved it, didn't I? In reality, the alcohol just compounded my anxiety. I had chest pains from the stress of it all—full-time work, young children who required so much, no time to exercise, no time to think or care about myself at all.

And as I read that blog on mommy wine culture, I found myself thinking not just about my own alcohol consumption, but about my family history.

I never met my grandfather, who was a police officer in the 1950s. He suffered from depression and alcohol addiction. One day, when my mom was about nine years old, a boy in her neighborhood ran up to her while she was playing outside and told her that her dad had just shot himself—the news must have swept through the neighborhood. She rushed home and found out it was true. My grandfather had ended his life with his police-issued revolver. It breaks my heart to imagine the trauma my mom experienced in that moment.

Growing up, we were told he died of cancer. Eventually, we were told he had cancer and was in so much pain that he took his own life. Finally, as adults, we learned the truth—he died by suicide after suffering severe depression and alcoholism. Maybe my mom should have told us the truth sooner, but the stigma was too much for her, and I don't envy her having to decide when and how to explain suicide to children. She buried her trauma and gave us a great childhood, but she cracked beneath the strain later.

All through my twenties, my mom suffered from depression and alcohol addiction. I spent a decade begging rehab facilities to take her in yet again, fighting with health insurance over coverage, calling 911 for help when she fell down the stairs, and screaming at her for all of the pain she was causing our family. After years of it, she finally found sobriety through AA. Our relationship has improved greatly, and she is back to her true self—a caring and generous mother and grandmother.

I thought of that pain that had rippled down through the generations, and I looked at my daughter—it was the week of her second birthday. *Yes, it's time to give this a try,* I thought.

I started the thirty-day Experiment and then became aware of *This Naked Mind*, which I bought and read in a couple of days. On page seventy-five, I stopped, my heart pounding as I read one line over and over: "It is much harder to go against the grain, skipping the drink and showing your children a different way, than it is to be swept along in our drinking culture. That is courage."

My choice to live alcohol-free wasn't just about me. It would impact my children and grandchildren. Alcohol had caused seventy years of trauma in my family. I had the power to stop it.

No more, I decided. *It ends here.*

It's been incredible. I've been proud of my good choices. I've despaired as I realized I had to relearn how to properly process my emotions without alcohol, that I didn't know how to address stress, anger, or even happiness without a drink in my hand. Through this process of learning so much about myself, my husband has been my rock-solid support. He never drank much, and I think my drinking always scared him—both for what it was and where it could lead. He's just finishing *This Naked Mind* now, and I think he won't ever drink again, either. We're in this together.

The days are beautiful now. Instead of being hungover on the weekends, I spend quality time with my husband and kids—biking, hiking, camping, exercising, cooking healthy meals, watching movies, playing games. We even took our first alcohol-free vacation this summer, and it was even more amazing than I could have imagined, from bonfires on the beach and rides on the boardwalk to great meals and sunsets over the ocean. Every moment was perfect. I would have lost so much of that precious time if I'd been drinking.

If there's anything I've learned, it's that alcohol holds us back from having the quality of life we yearn for. Now my interactions are authentic, my time with my family is meaningful, and my relationships are nurtured, as they should be.

I think of my grandfather sometimes, of how he didn't know that there was a better way. There was no one to show him the path out of the darkness that tormented him. I think of my mom, who walked that same road but survived. And I think of my children, who will never have to watch their parents face those demons, because I broke the generational legacy of addiction by saying alcohol has no place in my life. There are no words that can express the depth of my gratitude that there *was* someone to show me the path out while my children were still so young.

I watch my children run through the grass, innocent and carefree, with that all-encompassing childlike zest for life, and I'm reminded yet again that "thank you" will never be enough. But as I look forward to the future—not just mine, but theirs and their children's—I can't help but whisper it again: "Thank you. Thank you. Thank you."

"I like to say that I drink as much as I want, whenever I want. And the reality is that by knowing and reminding myself of the truth about alcohol, I haven't wanted a drink in years."

—Annie Grace, *The Alcohol Experiment*

CONCLUSION

It's been a wild ride!

Reading people's raw, vulnerable stories instills in me a deep sense of awe. In these pages, we've journeyed with each other through grief and love, pain and victory, loss and laughter.

We've walked alongside Bryan, who went from hopeless certainty that drinking would eventually kill him to absolute peace over the course of a single day, and with Ria, who discovered that she saved 11,000 calories and £240 every single month by not drinking.

We've celebrated with Ryan and Alison as they found freedom and fell in love again, and with Pamela as she rebuilt her life in the wake of tragedy.

We've marveled at the strength people have found within themselves, whether they'd hit their own personal rock bottom or not, to question their relationship with alcohol and break free from the trap they were caught in.

And maybe, in these stories, you've found reflections of yourself. I know I have. Simone said it perfectly: "When I listen to other people's stories, I find a little piece of myself in each of them—like

I'm a mosaic. And I hope that, by telling this story, other people can find a piece of themselves in it too."

I hope that you've discovered that you're not alone, that there is true joy and peace out there, and that you've found the treasure map that will lead you home.

If you're ready to take the next step in your journey and explore this freedom for yourself, I want to invite you to join our thirty-day Alcohol Experiment. All the proceeds from this book are earmarked to offset the ongoing costs of running The Alcohol Experiment, so that we can keep it forever free.

This Experiment is for you if you're curious about your relationship with alcohol. In these thirty days, you'll experience a taste of an alcohol-free life and explore some of the neuroscience behind why you might be drinking more than you want to, with no strings attached. You'll become a detached reporter, researching the facts, writing down your observations, and drawing your own conclusions. It's not a lifetime commitment—you're the only one who can decide if your life is better without alcohol. I'm willing to bet you'll enjoy the process!

With so much love,
Annie Grace

P.S. If you are ready to try an Alcohol Experiment of your own, you will find it forever free, thanks to this book, at: TheAlcoholExperiment.com.

THIS NAKED MIND
CONTROL ALCOHOL

A mind that no longer is at war with itself—agonizing about the decision to drink or not to drink.

This Naked Mind is a path to freedom from alcohol.

It's compiled from the **most cutting-edge research on alcohol in the disciplines of psychology and neurology**; it also examines the influence that alcohol has on our culture and society. It focuses on the dive into the roles of the conscious and unconscious mind in alcohol addiction, suggesting that a person's unconscious mind has been subjected to a lifetime of conditioning about the benefits of alcohol.

The process uses Liminal Thinking—a new approach that focuses on understanding how we construct and change our beliefs to help readers gain freedom from alcohol. You'll notice an interesting phenomenon taking place. **You won't want to drink anymore.** Yes, this really happens.

Rather than teaching you how to be sober, This Naked Mind takes the desire to drink away. Your desire to drink will be gone, so you won't feel like you are missing out. You aren't being deprived of anything.

The focus is not on staying sober, it is instead on just living and being happy.

You won't be pining for a drink or avoiding social situations because of temptation.

Without desire there exists no temptation.

> "Reading *This Naked Mind* has been nothing short of a miracle. It has helped me to see alcohol for what it is and ended a twenty-five-year cycle of binge drinking and 'trying' to stop or moderate . . . I feel happier, I'm regaining confidence, and my health is getting better every day. A must-read for anyone who wants to take control of their drinking but doesn't want a lifetime of struggle."—Kay W.

ThisNakedMind.com

Printed in Great Britain
by Amazon